CONTROL OVER PUBLIC FINANCE IN INDIA

About the Author

S.P. Ganguly belonged to the Indian Audit and Accounts Service. In 1985, he retired from the post of Commissioner-cum-Secretary, Finance Department, Government of Tripure, while holding the rank of Accountant General. He was the Chairman of the Pay Commission set up by the Government of Mizoram during 1990-1992.

CONTROL OVER PUBLIC FINANCE IN INDIA

Second Edition (Revised)

S.P. GANGULY
Ex-Chairman, Pay Commission
Mizoram

Foreword by
T.N. CHATURVEDI
(Former CAG of India & Union Home Secretary)

CONCEPT PUBLISHING COMPANY, NEW DELHI-110059

Cataloging in Publication Data—DK
Courtesy: D.K. Agencies (P) Ltd. <docinfo@dkagencies.com>

Ganguly, S. P., 1927-
Control over public finance in India / S.P. Ganguly ; foreword by T.N. Chaturvedi. — 2nd ed., rev.
p. cm.
Includes index.
ISBN 8180692914

1. Finance, Public—India. I. Title.

DDC 336.54 22

ISBN 81-8069-291-4

Second Edition (Revised), 2006
First Published 1997

Published and Printed by
Ashok Kumar Mittal
Concept Publishing Company
A/15-16, Commercial Block, Mohan Garden
New Delhi-110059 (INDIA)

Phones : 25351460, 25351794
Fax : 091-11-25357103
Email : publishing@conceptpub.com

To

Atish and Shiuli, Grandchildren;
Meenaksi and Enakshi, Daughters;
Kishore and Sanjoy, Sons-in-law
and
Pratima, Wife

Foreword

T.N. CHATURVEDI
M.P., Rajya Sabha
(Former CAG* of India & Union Home Secretary)

Finance, in its wider sense, is an exceedingly complex subject. But once its intricacies and interrelationships are unravelled, the matter no longer seems that difficult and abstruse. For any economy and polity, the question of resources in highly vital. The situation of competing needs and multiple requirements does exist even in affluent societies. That is why the maximisation of resources assumes paramount importance. In a democratic country and a society faced with imperatives of development, the need for greater attention to proper husbanding and utilisation of financial resources develops an added urgency. It is immaterial, in this context, whether the Government is activist or follows the policy of rolling back its activities.

Not many people are aware that during the alien dispensation, India's financial structure completely broke down after what we call the First War of Independence and the then rulers had to pay special thought to reorganisation of finances of the country and initiation of the system of financial control and audit which has now developed as the organisation of the CAG of India. But we are aware, after attainment of Independence and with the launching of planning, that the process of financial reforms has become a continuing function. It is not necessary to go into its details. As we are a union of states, it is of equal importance at both levels and also in their relationships.

Since we are committed to democratic parameters of the Constitution, the control of finance is not just ritualism. Accountability and transparency constitute its lifeblood. Propriety, equity, justice and integrity flow therefrom. Hence, it is of utmost importance that the financial system and its working are understood

---

* Comptroller and Auditor General of India

and followed scrupulously at all levels in the Government and administration if we want to strengthen the fabric of our democracy.

This book by Shri S.P. Ganguly is a highly welcome effort in the direction of adequate facilitation of easy comprehension of the working of the system in its wider framework. Shri Ganguly is a man of varied and extensive exprience of government functioning at different levels and a variety of institutional formations and organisations. In this slim volume, apart from introducing the theme and its relevance, he presents the political, government and administrative structure in the constitutional perspective and the evolutionary historical background. For him, control of finance is not only a technocratic exercise but a constitutional directive and a democratic compulsion. Shri Ganguly has explained scientifically, with lucidity and felicity of expression, the entire process of making of budget with its various stages and processes, proper utilisation of funds and the basic rules governing them so as to ensure responsiveness as well as accountability in administration. He throws light on the audit and its requirements of efficiency, economy, and effectiveness, as well as propriety and regularity and points out the role of audit, as the only aid to better management, improved performance, and effective administration. It has no adverse role if its functions are looked at with objectivity and dispassion. Shri Ganguly dwells on the role of the Public Accounts Committee and of the other Committee on Public Undertakings through which the Parliament is expected to discharge its onerous responsibility of holding the Executive and the administration accountable in conformity with aspirations and the mandate of the people. In this chain of public accountability, the CAG of India provides the vital link.

The book bears the deep imprint of Shri S.P. Ganguly's wide experience, extensive study and insight into the subject. I congratulate him for his signal service in widening the frontiers of the understanding of a difficult subject which is so vital to government functionaries, students of management and administration, legislators, and concerned citizens. It is an enlightening and exhilerating exposition of its theme.

I am appreciative of the honour the learned author and his enterprising publishers have done to me by inviting me to commend it to its perceptive readers.

26th July, 1996 T.N. CHATURVEDI

Preface to the Second Edition

With the passage of time the scenario of control over public finances has changed. Indeed, there is a growing opinion that the control has deteriorated. This book, therefore, has become even more relevant than when it was first published for those who are neither experts nor academics, and yet are interested in ensuring that public financial resources are judiciously utilised.

This book has been revised and updated. I do hope that it will be as extensively used, as was the earlier edition.

April, 2005

S.P. Ganguly

Preface

Public finance, for reasons well known, has become a matter of wide interest in the recent past. The mysteries of public finance have, however, remained mostly the exclusive preserve of the experts and academicians in the subject. In this book, I have made a very humble attempt to demystify the mysteries of public finance to meet the interest of those who are neither experts nor academicians in the subject and indicate what are the controls exercised over public finance in India and how those controls are exercised.

I am unable to find words to express my gratitude to Shri T.N. Chaturvedi, former Comptroller and Auditor General of India for the foreword he has kindly written for this book.

Calcutta
31st July, 1996

S.P. GANGULY

Acknowledgements

Books/Documents referred to:

1. Budget Documents, 1994-95
2. Constitution of India
3. Reports on Currency and Finance, Reserve Bank of India
4. General Financial Rules
5. Audit Code (First Edition, Second Reprint 1962)
6. An Introduction to Indian Government Accounts and Audit (Third Edition 1963)
7. Indian Administration (Second Edition), Ashok Chanda
8. Practice and Procedure of Parliament (Fourth Edition), Kaul & Sakhder
9. Golden Jubilee (1921-1971) Souvenir of the Public Accounts Committee
10. Fundamentals of Government Budgeting in India (Second Revised Edition 1993), S.P. Ganguly
11. Development and Communication in India (First Edition, 1992), G.N.S. Raghavan

Contents

1

Introductory

1.1 The meaning of the world 'Public' given in the Chamber's Twentieth Century Dictionary is "of a belonging to the people" or "pertaining to a community or nation." The meaning given in the same dictionary for the word 'Finance' is "money affairs or revenue especially of a ruler or state" or "public money". The expression "Public Finance" is thus finances of Government (both Central and State), which belong to the people or the nation as a whole.

1.2 India is a vast country. Its population in 2002-03 had crossed 120 crores. Apart from the Central Government, the Indian Republic has 28 State Governments and six Union Territory Governments. The Central Government and each of the State Governments have their accounts with the Reserve Bank of India, which is the banker of these Governments. The cash balance account of each of the State Governments and Central Government is separately maintained by the Reserve Bank of India. The inter-Government transactions are also adjusted by the Reserve Bank of India.

1.3 When the country gained independence on 15th August 1947, only the branches of the Reserve Bank of India and the Imperial Bank of India (predecessor of State Bank of India) used to conduct Government transactions wherever their branches existed. The branches of the Imperial Bank of India used to transact Government business, on behalf of the Reserve Bank of India, as its agent, wherever such branches existed. But such bank branches were very few and far between. Each district in India has a treasury called 'District Treasury', with Sub-Treasuries under it in each Sub-Division. [In Calcutta (now Kolkata), the office of the Accountant General, Bengal, now West Bengal, used to function as Treasury in passing bills for payment by the Reserve Bank of India branch in Kolkata]. These treasuries are the originating points, *i.e.*, the initial units of the fiscal system in India, as they render monthly accounts to the Accountant

General concerned for Government transactions, separately for Central and State Governments, after incorporating the transactions in Sub-Treasuries under each treasury. Before the banking system developed in the country, most of the Treasuries and Sub-treasuries also used to conduct cash transactions on behalf of the Central and the State Governments, unless there was any branch of the Reserve Bank of India or Imperial Bank of India at that station to conduct cash transactions on behalf of any treasury. With the nationalisation of banks and expansion of bank branches, now the treasuries and sub-treasuries are mostly linked to particular branches of public sector banks, which conduct cash transactions on behalf of the treasuries and sub-treasuries, on the basis of challans for depositing money and bills for payment of money passed by the treasuries and sub-treasuries. A few departments like Public Works Department, Forest Department are allowed to draw funds by cheques from the treasuries. It will thus appear that the fiscal administration in India is very complicated, if we consider not only the large number of units scattered all over the country, so far as the Central Government is concerned and all over the State in respect of a State Government's transactions, in which the transactions occur, but also the enormity of receipts and expenditure of the Central and State Governments. The budgetary transactions of the Central and State Governments were as follows in 2002-03 (Budget Estimates), as compared to 1983-84 (Budget Estimates); the figures for 1983-84 are given in brackets.

Receipts		*Disbursements*	
		Centre	
Revenue Receipts	253,935 (20,625)	Revenue Expenditure	366,227 (22,419)
Receipts on Capital Account	184,860 (13,453)	Disbursements on Capital Account	72,568 (13,213)
Total—Centre	438,795 (34,078)	Total (Centre)	438,795 (35,632)
		States	
Revenue Receipts	306,943 (23,665)	Revenue Expenditure	355,166 (22,602)
Receipts on Capital Account	118,812 (6,835)	Disbursement on Capital Account	75,768 (8,499)
Total—States	425,755 (30,506)	Total (States)	430,934 (31,101)
Total—Centre and States	864,550 (64,584)	Total	869,729 (66,733)

Sources: (1) Report on Currency, 2002-03 issued by the Reserve Bank of India (Tables 97, 99, 105, and 107).

(2) Report on Currency and Finance, 1982-83 issued by the Reserve Bank of India (Statements 78 and 82)

1.4 The process of distributing the cash balance of a Government between the different treasuries or paying units, so that each has sufficient funds to meet the local demand on it, is an intricate matter. The expression treasury here includes a bank branch which undertakes cash transactions on behalf of a treasury or sub-treasury under it. The collections in a treasury or a paying unit may be more than its requirement for making payments. Similarly, the requirement of funds in another treasury or paying unit may be much more than its collections. The arrangement for ensuring adequate cash balance in each treasury or paying unit at all times is, therefore, generally carried out by transferring cash from a surplus treasury to a deficit one or through the medium of currency chests. The currency chests are maintained on behalf of the Reserve Bank of India in treasuries or sub-treasuries (or in a bank branch which conducts cash transactions on behalf of treasury or sub-treasury). The Reserve Bank of India Act requires that the amount of currency or notes in circulation should not exceed certain limit (assets of the issue department of Reserve Bank). As such, a surplus treasury or paying unit transfers its surplus cash in the currency chest, while a deficit one draws cash from the currency chest for its requirements.

1.5 Consequent on separation of accounts from Audit in 1976, so far as Central Government is concerned, payments of Central Government are now made by the Pay and Accounts Offices under the Controller-General of Accounts, under the Ministry of Finance. They draw cheques on designated branches of Public Sector Banks to which they are linked.

1.6 The description given above of the fiscal arrangements in India for Government transactions briefly indicates how dispersed, diverse and complicated the same are.

1.7.1 In India, there are three-fold controls over public finance, *viz.*, (a) Parliamentary Control, (b) Administrative Control, and (c) Audit Control.

1.7.2 Parliamentary control is exercised in two stages. In the first stage, Parliamentary control is exercised at the time of policy making, as reflected in the annual budget. In the second stage, Parliamentary control is exercised *ex post facto* in ensuring that there has been no deviation in implementing the approved policy. Parliamentary control in the first stage is exercised at the time of approving the annual budget, which represents the financial policy of Government. Parliament's control is absolute in this regard, as under Article 266 of the Constitution no money out of the Consolidated Fund of India or the Consolidated Fund of a State shall be appropriated except in accordance with law and for the purposes and in the manner provided in the Constitution. The control in the second stage is exercised through the Public Accounts Committee and the Committee on Public Undertakings of the Parliament which consider the Reports of the Comptroller and Auditor General.

1.7.3 Administrative control is exercised at the time of preparation of the annual budget, which represents the policies of Government and for implementing which approval of Parliament is obtained through the annual budget. In the second stage, administrative control is exercised in regulating collection of receipts and incurring of expenditure in implementation of the will of the Parliament, *i.e.*, in implementing these policies reflected in the budget, which have received approval of Parliament.

1.7.4 Audit, which is independent of the Executive, is an important organ of Parliamentary democracy, like Judiciary. Briefly speaking, in exercising its scrutiny, Audit has to see how actually the financial policy of Government, as approved by Parliament, has been implemented according to the statutory provisions, and the rules, regulations and orders made thereunder. The scrutiny exercised by the Audit is *ex post facto*.

2

Administrative Structure in India and Structure of Audit Department

2.1 For the proper appreciation of administration of public finance in India, it would be better for us to briefly discuss the administrative structure in India, particularly because the administration of public finance is conducted through delegation of powers to functionaries at various levels of administration.

2.2.1 The provisions for the 'Executive' of the Union are contained in Chapter 1 of the Part V of the Constitution of India. Article 52 of the Constitution provides that "There shall be a President of India". The President is elected by members of the Council of States (Rajya Sabha), the House of the People (Lok Sabha) and the State Legislatures, for a period of 5 years, *vide* Articles 55 and 56 of the Constitution of India. Article 53 of the Constitution provides that the executive power of the Union shall be vested in the President and shall be exercised by him either directly or through officers subordinate to him in accordance with the Constitution.

2.2.2 The Constitution also provides for election of a Vice-President (Article 63) for five years (Article 67), who is the *ex-officio* chairman of the Council of States. Under Article 66 of the Constitution, the Vice-President is elected by the members of the Council of States and the House of the People. Under Article 65 of the Constitution, the Vice-President acts as President or discharges his functions during casual vacancies in the office or during the absence of the President, but unlike in the U.S.A., the Vice-President does not automatically become the President, when there is a permanent vacancy in the office. No executive power vests in him except as chairman of the Council of States.

2.2.3 Under Article 74 of the Constitution, "There shall be a Council of Ministers with the Prime Minister at the head to aid and advise the President who shall, in the exercise of his functions, act in accordance with such advice." Article 74 also provides that "the President may require the Council of Ministers to reconsider such advice, either generally, or otherwise, and the President shall act in accordance with the advice tendered after such reconsideration." Late Asok Chanda, a former Comptroller and Auditor General of India and an outstanding administrator of varied experience, expressed his view in his book *Indian Administration* (second edition), "The Indian Constitution is a comprehensive enactment defining the constitutional and administrative provisions in meticulous detail. The relations between the President and his government should, therefore, have been stated in more positive terms than the vague statement that there shall be a Council of Ministers to aid and advise him." He has cited two conflicting opinions expressed by constitutional experts of eminence. According to Late Patanjali Sastry, Ex-Chief Justice of India, "exercise of Presidential authority is limited over to the extent specifically mentioned in the Constitution." The other view cited by Asok Chanda is that of M.C. Setalvad, former Attorney General and supported by B.N. Rau, one time Adviser to the Constituent Assembly; according to their opinion the President has no functions to discharge on his own authority and he has merely "the right to be consulted, the right to encourage and the right to warn." The latter view has prevailed so far. Asok Chanda has mentioned in his book referred to above (p. 79) that "In fact, the first President seemed to have acquiesced in this position. Despite his known opposition to the Hindu Code Bill he refrained from sending any message to the House while the Bill was under discussion, and later from withholding his assent when the Bill was passed by both the Houses. Apart from any constitutional compulsion, this convention has thus come to be established by usage since the Constitution came into force." However, this question may come to fore again, if any bill violative of the provisions of the Constitution is passed by the both Houses of Parliament. If the President gives his assent to such a bill, he will be violating the Constitution, instead of being its protector.

2.2.4 Article 75 of the Constitution provides that : (i) the Prime Minister shall be appointed by the President and the other

Ministers shall be appointed by the President on the advice of the Prime Minister, (ii) the Ministers shall hold office during the pleasure of the President, and (iii) the Council of Ministers shall be collectively responsible to the House of the People. As the Constitution is very explicit on the point that the Council of Ministers is collectively responsible to the House of the People, the real executive power, exercisable by the Council of Ministers, flows from the House of the People. According to Asok Chanda, "The House of the People, representing the people, is supreme in the administration of the country. The Cabinet is merely its executive instrument." (*Indian Administration*, Second Edition, p. 50).

2.2.5 The Constitution does not have any provision specifying the duties and responsibilities of a Minister and his accountability to the Parliament, except the provisions of Article 78 of the Constitution, discussed later, about the duties of Prime Minister as respects the furnishing of information to President. But the provision in the Constitution that the Council of Ministers is collectively responsible to the House of the People clearly indicates that the Ministers derive their powers from the House of the People and they are fully accountable to it for their executive actions in respect of their respective departments. Article 77(3) of the Constitution provides that "the President shall make rules for the more convenient transactions of the business of the Government of India and for the allocation among Ministers of the said business." Under such statutory rules of allocation of business, a Minister is allocated a particular business of the Government of India and he thus is fully responsible for it. This question was dealt with by Justice M.C. Chagla who constituted the one-man commission to enquire into the certain investments made by the Life Insurance Corporation of India. Justice Chagla Commission observed that even if the actual responsibility for any improper and unjustified action lies with any officer in his Ministry, 'constitutionally the responsibility is that of the minister.' The Justice Chagla Commission concluded that "The Minister must take full responsibility for the acts of his subordinates. He cannot be permitted to say that his subordinates did not reflect his policy or acted contrary to his wishes or directions."

2.2.6 Article 78 of the Constitution provides that,

"It shall be the duty of the Prime Minister:

(a) to communicate to the President all decisions of the Council of Ministers relating to the administration of the affairs of the Union and proposals for legislation;
(b) to furnish such information relating to the administration of the affairs of the Union and proposals for legislation as the President may call for; and
(c) if the President so requires, to submit for the consideration of the Council of Ministers any matter on which a decision has been taken by a Minister but which has not been considered by the Council."

The above provisions enable the President to exercise his "right to be consulted, the right to encourage and the right to warn", as opined by M.C. Setalvad, supported by B.N. Rau, mentioned earlier in paragraph 2.2.3.

2.2.7 Article 78 of the Constitution also makes it clear that only the Prime Minister has access to the President, but none of his Ministers. Asok Chanda has stated that, "Constitutionally, therefore, the Prime Minister is the only link between the President and the Executive; no other minister can, as a matter of right, have an audience with the President" (*Indian Administration*, Second Edition, p.71).

2.2.8 Each Ministry has a secretariat headed by a Secretary. But there are cases in which a single Ministry has a number of departments, each of which has a secretariat headed by a Secretary. There is a Cabinet Secretary, the topmost bureaucrat of the country, who coordinates the activities of different Ministers/Departments through the respective Secretaries.

2.2.9 The most important organ of the present day bureaucracy is the office of the Prime Minister. Asok Chanda has observed that "Once the position is accepted that the real power of Government is vested in the Council of Ministers, subject only to parliamentary control, the logical corollary is reached that the Prime Minister is the repository of real power. The position of the Prime Minister in the Constitution of India is thus unique and his authority all pervading, in many ways, his powers are more extensive than those of the President of the United States of America. In addition to the exercise of the traditional powers of a Prime Minister in a Parliamentary democracy in the selection of his colleagues, allocation of portfolios, determination of the business of the Cabinet and constitution of Cabinet Committees and *ad hoc* committees, it is for him to nominate for the formal approval of the President, the Governors of the States and the Ambassadors and other diplomatic representatives of the country abroad." In this connection, Asok Chanda has drawn the following comparison:

"In the U.S.A., the Governors are elected and the Presidential nominations for diplomatic assignment have to be ratified by the Senate; the powers of the President are not so unfettered as the Prime Minister's in India." (*Indian Administration*, Second Edition, p. 82). It is no wonder, therefore, that Prime Minister's office acts as the trouble-shooter for the Prime Minister and has its clouts in every sphere of the Government of India.

2.2.10 It may be mentioned in this connection that by convention, the Finance Minister is responsible for the preparation of the budget. He obtains approval of the Prime Minister to his taxation proposals after discussions with him. The taxation proposals are divulged to the Cabinet only on its day of presentation of the budget to the Parliament.

2.2.11 The administration of the country is conducted through delegations of power to different units of bureaucracy. It has been mentioned earlier that under Article 77(3) of the Constitution, the President shall make rules for the more convenient transaction of the business of the Government of India, and for the allocation among Ministers of the said business. The delegations are made on the basis of the rules framed under Article 77(3) of the Constitution. Under these rules, the Minister delegates his powers to his junior ministerial colleague or junior ministerial colleagues, the Secretary and other officials in the Secretariat.

2.2.12 Outside the Secretariat there are Heads of Departments and their field officers of various grades. For example, under the Ministry of Health, there is a Director General of Health Services. Under the Director General of Health Services, there are central hospitals and dispensaries of different grades, apart from his field offices at different regions and States, not only for general health services but also for different schemes like Leprosy, Malaria, etc., for co-ordination of work to be executed by the different State Governments. In some cases, the head of the office in a field office is only a gazetted officer in Group B of Central Services. The officers function with financial powers delegated under the Delegation of Financial Powers Rules, 1958 subject to the following reservations in the General Financial Rules (GRFs):

(i) The financial powers of Government, which have not been delegated to a subordinate authority, shall vest in the Finance Ministry. (GFR 34)

(ii) Unless otherwise provided by any special rule of order it shall be within the competence of an authority to exercise the financial powers delegated to another authority subordinate to it. (GFR 35)

(iii) Except in pursuance of the general delegation made by, or with the approval of the President, a subordinate authority shall not, without the previous consent of the Finance Ministry, issue an order, which:

(a) involves any grant of land or assignment of revenue, or concession, grant, lease or licence of mineral or forest right or right to water power or any easement or privilege in respect of such concessions, or

(b) involves relinquishment of revenue in anyway. (GFR 36)

The delegations are such that while certain things may require the approval of the Cabinet, some other smaller things may be sanctioned by a Head of office in the rank of a Group B officer.

STATE

2.3.1 The provisions for the executive of the States are contained in Chapter II of Part VI of the Constitution. Under Article 153 of the Constitution, "There shall be a Governor for each State", who is appointed by the President for five years under Article 156 of the Constitution. Article 154 of the Constitution provides that "The executive power of the State shall be vested in the Governor and shall be exercised by him either directly or through officers subordinate to him in accordance with this Constitution." All executive actions of the Government of State shall be expressed to be taken in the name of the Governor (Article 166 of the Constitution).

2.3.2 Under Article 163 of the Constitution in each State, "There shall be a Council of Ministers with the Chief Minister at the head to aid and advise the Governor in the exercise of his functions, except in so far as he is by or under this Constitution required to exercise his functions or any of them in his discretion." It may be noticed here that so far as the discretionary powers vested in the Governor under the Constitution are concerned, the Governor is not bound by the advice of the Council of Ministers, but is to act independently.

2.3.3 As in the case of Prime Minister in his relation with the President, it is the duty of Chief Minister of a State under Article 167 of the Constitution, (i) to communicate to the Governor of State all decisions of the Council of Ministers relating to the administration of the affairs of the State and proposals for legislation, (ii) to furnish such information relating to the administration of the affairs of the State and proposals for legislation as the Governor may call for, and (iii) if the Governor so requires, to submit for the consideration of the Council of Ministers any matter on which a decision has been taken by a Minister but which has not been considered by the Council of Ministers.

2.3.4 Under Article 166(3) of the Constitution, "The Governor shall make rules for the more convenient transaction of the business of the Government of the State, and for allocation among Ministers of the said business, in so far as it is not business with respect to which the Governor is by or under this Constitution required to act in his discretion."

2.3.5 The Chief Secretary is at the top of the bureaucracy in a State, followed by Secretaries of each Department. As in the case of the Centre, there are various offices of different grades under each Department, starting from a Head of Department to Heads of offices, who are, in most cases, officers of Group B of the Stale Civil Service, at the lowest level of gazetted officers. As in the case of the Centre, the executive functions are carried out by the officers of different grades under powers delegated to them, both executive and financial. Thus, while certain matters may require the approval of the Council of Ministers, certain other powers may be exercised even by a gazetted officer of Group B of State Civil Service under delegated powers.

2.4 In the context of administration of Public Finance in India, we have necessarily to include in the administrative structure of the country, (i) the Finance Commission, and (ii) the Planning Commission, as they play very important roles in dealing with Public Finance in India.

2.5.1 Under Article 280 of the Constitution a Finance Commission is set up by the President. The provisions of Article 280 are as follows:

"(1) The President shall, within two years from the commencement of this Constitution and thereafter at the expiration of every fifth year or at such earlier time as the President considers necessary, by order constitute a Finance Commission which shall consist of a Chairman and four other members to be appointed by the President.

(2) Parliament may by law determine the qualifications which shall be requisite for appointment as members of the Commission and the manner in which they shall be selected.

(3) It shall be the duty of the Commission to make recommendations to the President as to:

(a) The distribution between the Union and States of the net proceeds of taxes which are to be, or may be, divided between them under this chapter and the allocation between the States of the respective shares of such proceeds;

(b) the principles which should govern the grants-in-aid of the revenues to the States out of the Consolidated Fund of India;

(c) any other matter referred to the Commission by the President in the interests of sound finance.

(4) The Commission shall determine their procedures and shall have such powers in the performance of their functions as Parliament may by law confer on them."

2.5.2 Under Article 280(3)(c) of the Constitution several matters other than the principles governing devolution of taxes and payment of grants to States are referred to each Finance

Commission. The recommendations of each Finance Commission are, therefore, of great importance for Public Finance in India.

2.6.1 While the Finance Commission is a creature of the Constitution, the Planning Commission is not so. The Planning Commission was constituted in March 1950. The Prime Minister is the Chairman of the Planning Commission. The resources of the country being limited, the Planning Commission was given the responsibility for making realistic assessment of the resources and their appropriate utilisation, after determining the priorities as between plans and programmes for balanced development of the country.

2.6.2 Asok Chanda had observed in his book *Indian Administration* (second edition, p. 96) that, "the place of the Commission in India's administration and its relations with both the Central and State Governments were not, however, clearly stated." He went on to say, "It would be only stating the obvious to say that the determination of policy and the objectives which it has to fulfil must necessarily be the primary function of the Cabinet accountable to Parliament. Equally, the unhampered execution of accepted plans and programmes must be the responsibility of the departments. These functions could hardly be shared with any other authority," and "The position of pre-eminence accorded to the Planning Commission is inconsistent with the conception of a Cabinet form of Government. Nor is the present quasi-political composition of Commission wholly suitable for the purpose of giving shape and form to policies and objectives laid down by the Cabinet." The Planning Commission assisted by its team of technical officials, has, however, been able to establish its niche in the Indian administrative structure, as an useful tool for not only finalising the five year plans and the annual plans but also as the agency coordinating the planning efforts of the Centre and the States. The manner in which it discharges this role will be discussed later while dealing with executive control of public finance. Broadly, however, while the Finance Commission's recommendations are in respect of non-Plan account, it is the role of the Planning Commission to determine the developmental needs in the case of both the Union Government and the States, in finalising the 'Plan' for approval of the National Development Council.

Structure of Audit Department

2.7.1 Under Article 148(1) of the Constitution, there shall be a Comptroller and Auditor General of India who shall he appointed by the President by warrant under his hand and seal and shall be removed from office in like manner and on the grounds as a judge of the Supreme Court. If this is read with Article 124(4) of the Constitution, the Comptroller and Auditor General of India can be removed from his office only by an order of the President passed after an address by each House of Parliament supported by a majority of the total membership of that House and by a majority of not less than two-thirds of the members of that House present and voting has been presented to the President in the same session for such removal on the ground of proved misbehaviour or incapacity.

The expenditure on salary, allowances and pension payable to or in respect of the Comptroller and Auditor General of India is charged on the Consolidated Fund of India under Article 112(3)(e) of the Constitution. Neither the salary of a Comptroller and Auditor General nor his rights of leave of absence, pension or age of retirement shall be varied to his disadvantage after his appointment *vide* proviso to Article 148(3) of the Constitution. Article 148(6) of the Constitution provides that the administrative expenses of the office of the Comptroller and Auditor General, including all salaries, allowances and pensions payable to or in respect of persons serving in that office shall be charged upon the Consolidated Fund of India. In other words, the expenditure on his salary, allowances and pension, similar expenditure on persons working in his office and also the administrative expenses in his office shall not be submitted to the vote of the Parliament.

2.7.2 Under Article 151 of the Constitution, the reports of the Comptroller and Auditor General relating to the accounts of the Union shall be submitted to the President, who shall cause them to be laid before each House of Parliament. Similarly, the reports of the Comptroller and Auditor General relating to the accounts of a State shall he submitted to the Governor of the State, who shall cause them 10 be laid before the Legislature of the State.

2.7.3 Under Article 149 of the Constitution, the Comptroller and Auditor General shall perform such duties and exercise such powers in relation to the accounts of the Union and of the States and of any other authority or body as may be prescribed by or under any law made by Parliament. The Comptroller and Auditor General's (Duties, Powers and Conditions of Service) Act, 1971 came into force on 15th December 1971. Till then the Comptroller and Auditor General exercised the duties and powers, which he used to exercise under the Government of India (Audit and Accounts) Order, 1936 as adopted by the India (Provisional Constitution) Order, 1947. The Comptroller and Auditor General's (Duties, Powers and Conditions of Service) Act, 1971, has been amended in 1976, 1984 and 1987.

2.7.4 Under the Comptroller an Auditor General's (Duties, Powers and Conditions of Service) Act, 1971, his duties, in the main, are as follows:

(i) Under Section 10 of the Act, as amended in 1976, the Comptroller and Auditor General has been relieved of responsibility for keeping the accounts of the Union Government, except for : (a) transactions relating to pensions of the Indian Audit and Accounts Department, (b) provident fund accounts of all employees of the Indian Audit and Accounts Department, and (c) Union Territories of Chandigarh, Lakshadweep and Dadra and Nagar Havelli.

(ii) The Comptroller and Auditor General is responsible for keeping the accounts of the States except for Goa. However, he has been relieved of the responsibility for maintaining the Provident Fund Accounts of all State Government employees of Rajasthan, Mizoram, Arunachal Pradesh, Jammu & Kashmir, Bihar and Punjab.

(iii) Appropriation Accounts are prepared by the authorities which keep the accounts. As such, the Comptroller and Auditor General is no longer required to prepare the Appropriation Accounts of Union Government. The Appropriation Accounts for the States are, however, prepared by him, except for Goa.

(iv) Under Section 11 of the Act, he has been relieved of the responsibility for the preparation of the Finance Accounts of the Union Government from 1977-78 onwards by an order issued by the President in June 1978. He was also relieved of the responsibility for preparation of the Finance Accounts of the Union Territory of Pondicherry since 1988-89, by an order issued by the President under Section 11 of the Act. He, however, continues to prepare the Finance Accounts of the State Government except for Goa. He was relieved of the responsibility for the preparation of the Finance Accounts of Goa since 1988-89 by an order issued by the Governor of Goa, with the previous approval of the President, under Section 11 of the Act.

2.7.5 As regards audit, the duties of the Comptroller and Auditor General under the Comptroller and Auditor General's (Duties, Powers and Conditions of Service) Act, 1971, are as follows:

(i) Section 13. *General provisions relating to audit.*

"It shall be the duty of the Comptroller and Auditor General—

(a) to audit all expenditure from the Consolidated Fund of India and of each State and of each Union Territory having a Legislative Assembly and to ascertain whether the moneys shown in the accounts as having been disbursed were legally available for and applicable to the service or purpose to which they have been applied or charged and whether the expenditure conforms to the authority which governs it;

(b) to audit all transactions of the Union and of the States relating to Contingency Funds and Public Accounts;

(c) to audit all trading, manufacturing, profit and loss accounts and balance-sheets and other subsidiary accounts in any department of the Union or of a State;

and in each case to report on the expenditure, transactions or accounts so audited by him."

(ii) Section 14. *Audit of receipts and expenditure of bodies or authorities substantially financed from Union or State Revenues.*

"(1) Where anybody or authority is substantially financed by grants or loans from the Consolidated Fund of India or of any State or of any Union Territory having a Legislative Assembly, the Comptroller and Auditor General shall, subject to the provisions of any law for the time being in force applicable to the body or authority, as the case may be, audit all receipts and expenditure of that body or authority and to report on the receipts and expenditure audited by him.

Explanation.—Where the grant or loan to a body or authority from the Consolidated Fund of India or of any State or of any Union Territory having a Legislative Assembly in a financial year is not less than rupees twenty-five lakhs and the amount of such grant or loan is not less than seventy-five per cent of the total expenditure of that body or authority, such body or authority shall be deemed, for the purposes of this sub-section, to be substantially financed by such grants or loans as the case may be.

(2) Notwithstanding anything contained in sub-section (1) the Comptroller and Auditor General may with the previous approval of the President or the Governor of a State or the Administrator of a Union Territory having a Legislative Assembly, as the case may be, audit all receipts and expenditure of anybody or authority where the grants or loans to such body or authority from the Consolidated Fund of India or of any State or of any Union Territory having a Legislative Assembly, as the case may be, in a financial year is not less than rupees one crore.

(3) Where the receipts and expenditure of anybody or authority are by virtue of the fulfilment of the conditions specified in sub-section (1) or sub-section (2) audited by the Comptroller and Auditor General in a financial year, he shall continue to audit the receipts and expenditure of that body or authority for a further period of two years notwithstanding that the conditions specified in sub-section (1) or sub-section (2) are not fulfilled during any of the two subsequent years."

(iii) Section 15. *Functions of Comptroller and Auditor General in the case of grants or loans given to the other authorities or bodies.*

"(1) Where any grant or loan is given for any specific purpose from the Consolidated Fund of India or of any State or any Union Territory having a Legislative Assembly to any authority or body, not being a foreign State or international organisation, the Comptroller and Auditor General shall scrutinise the procedures by which the sanctioning authority satisfies itself as to the fulfilment of the conditions subject to which such grants or loans were given and shall for this purpose have right of access, after giving reasonable notice, to the books and accounts of that authority or body:

Provided that the President, the Governor of a State or the Administrator of a Union Territory having a Legislative Assembly, as the case may be, may, where he is of opinion that it is necessary so to do in the public interest, by order, relieve the Comptroller and Auditor General after consultation with him, from making any such scrutiny in respect of anybody or authority receiving such grant or loan.

(2) Except where he is authorized so to do by the President, the Governor of a State or the Administrator of a Union Territory having a Legislative Assembly, as the case may be, the Comptroller and Auditor General shall not have while exercising the powers conferred on him by sub-section (1), right of access to the books and accounts of any corporation to which any such grant or loan as is referred to in sub-section (1) is given if the law by or under which such corporation has been established provides for the audit of the accounts of such corporation by an agency other than the Comptroller and Auditor General:

Provided that no such authorization shall be made except after consultation with the Comptroller and Auditor General and except after giving the concerned corporation a reasonable opportunity of making representations with regard to the proposal to give to the Comptroller and Auditor General right of access to its books and accounts."

(iv) Section 16. *Audit of Receipts of Union or of States.*

"It shall be the duty of the Comptroller and Auditor General to audit all receipts which are payable into Consolidated Fund of India and of each State and of each Union Territory having a Legislative Assembly and to satisfy himself that the rules and procedures in that behalf are designed to secure an effective check on the assessment, collection and proper allocation of revenue and are being duly observed and to make for this purpose such examination of the accounts as he thinks fit and report thereon."

(v) Section 17. *Audit of Accounts of Stores and Stock.*

"The Comptroller and Auditor General shall have authority to audit and report on the accounts of stores and stock kept in any office or department of the Union or of a State."

2.7.6 The powers of the Comptroller and Auditor General in connection with audit of accounts, under the Comptroller and Auditor General's (Duties, Powers and Conditions of Service) Act, 1971, are as follows:

Section 18. "(1) The Comptroller and Auditor General shall in connection with the performance of his duties under this Act, have authority:

(a) to inspect any office of accounts under the control of the Union or of a State, including treasuries and such offices responsible for the keeping of initial or subsidiary accounts, as submit accounts to him;
(b) to require that any accounts, books, papers and other documents which deal with or form the basis of or are otherwise relevant to the transactions to which his duties in respect of audit extend, shall be sent to such place as he may appoint for inspection;

(c) to put such questions or make such observations as he may consider necessary, to the person in charge of the office and to call for such information as he may require for the preparation of any account or report which is his duty to prepare.

(2) The person in charge of any office or department, the accounts of which have to be inspected and audited by the Comptroller and Auditor General, shall afford all facilities for such inspection and comply with requests for information in as complete a form as possible and with all reasonable expedition."

2.7.7 The duties and powers of the Comptroller and Auditor General, under the Comptroller and Auditor General's (Duties, Power and Conditions of Service) Act, 1971, in relation to audit of Government Companies and Corporations are as follows:

Section 19

"(1) The duties and powers of the Comptroller and Auditor General in relation to the audit of the accounts of Government companies shall be performed and exercised by him in accordance with the provisions of the Companies Act, 1956 (1 of 1956).

(2) The duties and powers of the Comptroller and Auditor General in relation to the audit of the accounts of corporations (not being companies) established by or under law made by Parliament shall be performed and exercised by him in accordance with the provisions of the respective legislation.

(3) The Governor of a State or the Administrator of a Union Territory having a Legislative Assembly may, where he is of opinion that it is necessary in the public interest so to do, request the Comptroller and Auditor General to audit the accounts of a corporation established by law made by the Legislature of the State or of the Union Territory, as the case may be, and where such request has been made, the Comptroller and Auditor General shall audit the accounts of such corporation and shall

have, for the purposes of such audit, right of access to the books and accounts of such corporation:

Provided that no such request shall be made except after consultation with the Comptroller and Auditor General and except after giving reasonable opportunity to the corporation to make representations with regard to the proposal for such audit."

Section 19A. *Laying of reports in relation to accounts of Government companies and corporations.*

"(1) The reports of the Comptroller and Auditor General in relation to the accounts of a Government company or corporation referred to in Section 19, shall be submitted to the Government or Governments concerned.

(2) The Central Government shall cause every report received by it under sub-section (1) to be laid, as soon as may be, after it is received, before each House of Parliament.

(3) The State Government shall cause every report received by it under sub-section (1) to be laid, as soon as may be, after it is received, before the Legislative of the State.

Explanation.—For the purpose of this section 'Government' or 'State Government' in relation to a Union territory having a Legislative Assembly, means the Administrator of the Union territory."

2.7.8 The provisions for audit of accounts of certain authorities or bodies, not mentioned earlier, in the Comptroller and Auditor General's (Duties, Powers and Conditions of Service) Act, 1971 are as follows:

Section 20

"(1) Save as otherwise provided in Section 19, where the audit of the accounts of anybody or authority has not been entrusted to the Comptroller and Auditor General by or under any law made by Parliament, he shall, if requested so to do by the President, or the Governor of a State or the Administrator of a Union Territory having a

Legislative Assembly, as the case may be, undertake the audit of the accounts of such body or authority on such terms and conditions as may be agreed upon between him and the concerned Government and shall have for the purposes of such audit, right of access to the books and accounts of that body or authority:

Provided that no such request shall be made except after consultation with the Comptroller and Auditor General.

(2) The Comptroller and Auditor General may propose to the President or the Governor of a State or the Administrator of a Union Territory having a Legislative Assembly, as the case may be, that he may be authorized to undertake the audit of the accounts of anybody or authority, the audit of accounts of which has not been entrusted to him by law, if he is of the opinion that such audit is necessary because a substantial amount has been invested in, or advanced to such body or authority by the Central or State Government or by the Government of a Union Territory having a Legislative Assembly, and on such request being made, the President or the Governor or the Administrator, as the case may be, may empower the Comptroller and Auditor General to undertake the audit of the accounts of such body or authority.

(3) The audit referred to in sub-section (1) or sub-section (2) shall not be entrusted to the Comptroller and Auditor General except where the President or the Governor of a State or the Administrator of Union Territory having a Legislative Assembly, as the case may be, is satisfied that it is expedient so to do in the public interest and except after giving a reasonable opportunity to the concerned body or authority to make representations with regard to the proposal for such audit."

2.7.9 The Constitution and the Comptroller and Auditor General's (Duties, Powers and Conditions of Service) Act, 1971 have adequate provisions to ensure that the Comptroller and Auditor General is able to discharge his functions and duties and exercise his powers fearlessly, with independence and dignity. It is for the incumbent of the post to uphold the dignity and, independence of that post with his honesty, impartiality and objectivity.

In his own office, the Comptroller and Auditor General is assisted by two Deputy Comptrollers and Auditors General. One Deputy Comptroller and Auditor General is also the chairman of the Audit Board for the Central Public Sector Undertakings. There are also five Additional Deputy Comptroller and Auditors General and several other officers of the rank of Principal Accountant General, Accountant General, Senior Deputy Accountant General and Deputy Accountant General in his office, who are assisted by a number of Administrative officers and subordinate staff.

For the separated audit offices, there are a number of field officers of the ranks of Directors General of Audit and Principal Directors of Audit, who head those offices. The Audit and Account Offices relating to accounts of States are headed by officers of the rank of Principal Accountant General or Accountant General.

Since the Accountants General of States are responsible for keeping and compilation of accounts, audit is conducted both centrally in the respective offices of the Accountants General with reference to treasury challans for receipts and vouchers for payments and locally in the offices of the State Governments with reference to the initial records. In the cases of Union Government, Government bodies or organisations which maintain their accounts and non-Government organisations, audit is conducted by local inspection of the offices with reference to the receipts, vouchers and other initial records.

3

Public Finance

3.1 The Constitutional provisions relating to public finance are discussed below.

3.2.1 Consolidated Fund

The Consolidated Fund has been defined in Article 266(1) of the Constitution. According to the same, all revenues received by the Government of India, all loans raised by that Government by the issue of treasury bills, loans or ways and means advances and all moneys received by that Government in repayment of loans shall form one consolidated fund to be entitled "The Consolidated Fund of India", and all revenues received by the Government of a State, all loans raised by that Government by the issue of treasury bills, loans or ways and means advances and all moneys received by that Government in repayment of loans shall form one consolidated fund to be entitled "The Consolidated Fund of the State."

3.2.2 Under Article 266(3) of the Constitution, no moneys out of the Consolidated Fund of India or the Consolidated Fund of a State shall be appropriated except in accordance with law and for the purposes and in the manner provided in the Constitution.

3.2.3 The following Chart indicates the main divisions of the Consolidated Fund.

3.3.1 Public Account

According to the definition given in Article 266(2) of the Constitution, all public moneys, other than those related to the Consolidated Fund of the Government of India or the Government

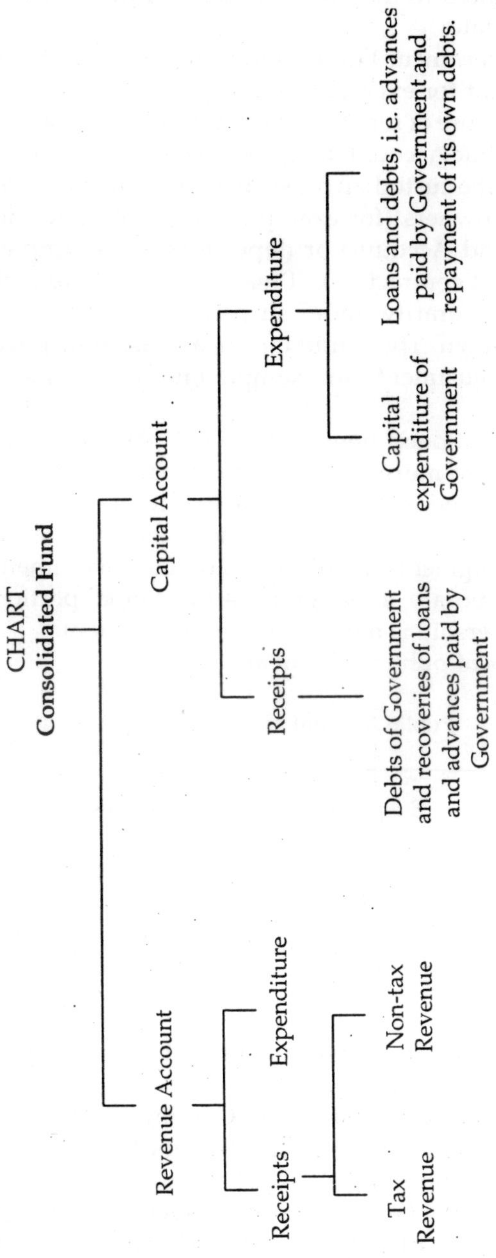
CHART
Consolidated Fund
Revenue Account
Capital Account
Receipts
Expenditure
Tax Revenue
Non-tax Revenue
Receipts
Expenditure
Debts of Government and recoveries of loans and advances paid by Government
Capital expenditure of Government
Loans and debts, i.e. advances paid by Government and repayment of its own debts.

of a State shall be credited to the public account of India or the public account of the State.

Except for the Government Funds held in Reserve Funds or deposits by Government for expenditure on specified objects or the moneys held in suspense or remittance account for adjustments, other moneys in the Public Account do not belong to Government. Government is merely the custodian for such moneys till these are repaid to the rightful owners (for example, contributors to the General Provident Fund Account) or depositors (for example, deposits of Government contractors). It may be added here that an amount is held temporarily under suspense when its exact classification is not known. The remittance heads are transitory heads pending final adjustment, for example inter-Government transactions.

3.3.2 It may be mentioned here that the net balance in the public account remains merged in the cash balance of the Government concerned and is thus available to it for its own use like any other borrowed funds and to that extent, the net balance in the public account augments the resources of the Government concerned, even if temporary, although for a substantial portion of the net balance ownership is not that of the Government.

3.3.3 The divisions of public account are as follows:

Public Account

- Debts (other than those included in Consolidated Fund), reserve funds, deposits etc.
- Suspense
- Remittances

3.4 Contingency Fund

Article 267 of the Constitution defines Contingency Fund as follows:

(1) Parliament may by law establish a Contingency Fund in the nature of an imprest to be entitled "the Contingency Fund of India" into which shall be paid from time to time such sums as may be determined by such law, and the said Fund shall be placed at the disposal of the President

said Fund shall be placed at the disposal of the President to enable advances to be made by him out of such Fund for the purposes of meeting unforeseen expenditure pending authorisation of such expenditure by Parliament by law under Article 115 or Article 116.

(2) The Legislature of a State may by law establish a Contingency Fund in the nature of an imprest to be entitled "the Contingency Fund of the State" into which shall be paid from time to time such sums as may be determined by such law, and the said Fund shall be placed at the disposal of the Governor of the State to enable advances to be made by him out of such Fund for the purposes of meeting unforeseen expenditure pending authorisation of such expenditure by the Legislature of the State by law under Article 205 or Article 206.

3.5 Articles 268 to 279 of the Constitution relate to distribution of revenues between the Union and States, for example, duties levied by the Union but collected and appropriated by the States, taxes levied and collected by the Union but assigned to the States, taxes levied and collected by the Union and distributed between the Union and the States, etc.

3.6 Articles 282 to 290-A contain miscellaneous financial provisions, such as, expenditure defrayable by the Union or a State out of its revenues, custody of Consolidated Funds, Contingency Funds and money credited to the public accounts, custody of suitors' deposits and other moneys received by public servants and courts, etc.

3.7 Government Borrowings and Guarantees

3.7.1 Under Article 292 of the Constitution, the executive power of the Union extends to borrowing upon the security of the Consolidated Fund of India within such limits, if any, as may from time to time be fixed by Parliament by law and to the giving of guarantees within such limits, if any as may be so fixed.

3.7.2 Similarly, under Article 293 of the Constitution, a State Government may borrow within the territory of India upon the security of the Consolidated Fund of the State within such limits, if any, as may from time to time be fixed by the Legislature of such

State by law and to the giving of guarantees within such limits, if any, as may be fixed.

3.7.3 Neither the Parliament nor any State Legislature has fixed any limit for borrowing or giving guarantee. But although the Central Government may borrow or give guarantee without any restriction, no State Government is free to do so, as Article 293(3) provides that a State Government which is indebted to the Central Government, will have to obtain consent of the Central Government for raising any loan, and there is no State Government which is not indebted to the Central Government. The other restriction in the case of a State Government is that it can raise loan only within the country and cannot take any loan directly from outside the country. All foreign loans are, therefore, raised by the Government of India and re-lent to the State Governments, for specific programmes and projects.

3.8 The following transactions are out-flows from or in-flows to the Consolidated Fund:

(i) Investments in and grants or loans to Government companies or corporations (not being companies) established under specific laws, dividends, if any received from them, repayment of loans by them and interest received on such loans.

(ii) Grants or loans to autonomous statutory bodies or registered bodies set up by Government, repayment of such loans and interest received on such loans.

(iii) Investments in and grants or loans to cooperatives, registered societies, various private and non-Government institutions, organisations or bodies (for example, voluntary social organisations, private educational institutions, voluntary service organisations, etc.) dividends, if any, received from them, repayment of loans by them and interest received on such loans.

Except to the extent of investments made and grants or loans paid from the Consolidated Fund, dividend, if any, received on investments, repayment of loans and interest received on such loans, which are credited to the Consolidated Fund, the transactions of the above mentioned Government Companies and Corporations, other statutory bodies set up by Government, registered societies set up by Government, various private and non-Government organisations, societies, institutions, bodies or cooperatives, etc., are outside the Consolidated Fund. But their transactions being outside the Consolidated Fund does not take them away from the scope and extent of public finance. The transactions of the Government Companies and Corporations and other bodies set up by Government as mentioned in (i) and (ii) above fall fully within the ambit of public finance. Even the transactions of those falling under (iii) above, are linked with the Interest of public finance, as efficient management of their transactions can only ensure proper utilisation of funds made available to them from the Consolidated Fund for the purpose for which they have been made available, receipt of adequate return on investments in them, repayment of loans by them and receipt of interest from them on the loans paid to them. That is why provisions have been made for audit of their transactions in Sections 14, 15, 19 and 20 of the Comptroller and Auditor General's (Duties, Powers and Conditions of Service) Act, 1971. In fact, in the cases of Government Companies and Corporations, other statutory bodies and registered societies etc., set up by Government as mentioned in (i) and (ii) above, the scope and extent of public finance extend much beyond their own transactions. For example, a public sector bank advances money to a private sector company. The interest of public finance is affected, if the private sector company does not perform well and fails to repay the money with interest to the public sector bank. It is, therefore, not enough only to provide for a system to regulate and monitor the working of the public sector banks and the payment of advances by public sector banks to private sector companies; it is equally important to provide for a system under which the financing banks are responsible for monitoring the transactions of the private sector companies for safeguarding the interest of public finance. This is only an example. There are numerous such areas which require appropriate and adequate systems for safeguarding the interest of public finance.

3.9 Classification

3.9.1 Classification of transactions relating to public finance is of utmost importance, as such classification of a transaction indicates a particular activity of Government, and also its nature and purpose.

3.9.2 In the Constitution itself, expenditure has been classified as 'charged' and 'voted'. In the case of the Union Government, the items of expenditure which shall be charged on the Consolidated Fund of India have been indicated in Article 112(3) of the Constitution. Similarly, items of expenditure which shall be charged on the Consolidated Fund of a State have been indicated in Article 202(3) of the Constitution. Such items of expenditure charged on the Consolidated Fund of India or the Consolidated Fund of State shall not be submitted to the vote of the Parliament or the State Legislature, as the case may be, *vide* Article 113(1) and Article 203(1) of the Constitution, while all other items of expenditure are required to be submitted to the vote of the Parliament or the State Legislature, in the form of demands for grants under Article 113(2) and Article 203(2) of the Constitution respectively.

3.9.3 Under Article 150 of the Constitution, the accounts of Union and of the States shall be kept in such form as the President may, on the advice of the Comptroller and Auditor General of India, prescribe. The heads of classification (Sectors, Major Heads and Minor Heads of classification) of Government transactions have been prescribed by the Union Government on the advice of the Comptroller and Auditor General of India. The State Governments have no power to prescribe such heads of classification. This ensures uniformity in accounts of the Union Government and the State Governments. There is also substantial inter-relation between the accounts of the Central Government and the State Governments because of transfer of resources from Centre to States.

3.9.4 Such uniformity in accounts of the Union and the State Governments makes it possible to prepare the Combined Finance and Revenue Accounts for each financial year showing the receipts and expenditure up to the level of Minor Heads for the Union Government, each of the State Governments and the grand total for the entire country. Progress in capital expenditure and outstanding liabilities are also shown in the Combined Finance and Revenue Accounts. The combined Finance and Revenue Accounts of each year is prepared on the basis of the annual accounts called "Finance Accounts" of the Central Government and the State Governments submitted to the Parliament and the respective State Legislature. The combined Finance and Revenue

Accounts enable inter-Government comparison of receipts and expenditure under different Sectors. Major Heads and Minor Heads, for which it is considered a very useful document.

3.9.5 The five-tier arrangement for classification of Government transactions is indicated below:

Sector
↓
Major Heads
↓
Minor Heads
↓
Sub-Heads
↓
Detailed-Heads

Some of the Sectors are divided into Sub-sectors. Each Major Head is divided into a number of Minor Heads. In some cases, there are Sub-Major Heads under a Major Head. The Sub-Heads under a Minor Head are divided into Detailed Heads.

Each Sector, such as Social Services, Economic Services, General Services, etc., represents a group of functions or services of Government. For example, expenditure on general education, technical education, art and culture, medical and public health, family welfare etc. are treated as functions under Social Services. Expenditure on agriculture and allied activities, industry and minerals, transport and communications, energy etc., are functions under Economic Services. General Services include expenditure on organs of State, fiscal services, interest payment and servicing of debt, administrative services, etc. Each Major Head represents a function or service. Examples of Major Heads representing the functions or services are, 2202 General Education, 2403 Animal Husbandry, 2801 Power, 2049 Interest Payments, etc. The Minor Heads subordinate to the Major Heads identify the programmes for achieving the objectives of the function or service represented by the Major Heads. Sub-Heads under a Minor Head indicate schemes and activities under a programme. However, if any programme represents non-developmental expenditure or expenditure of administrative nature, a Sub-Head usually represents a component of the programme. The Detailed Heads representing standard objects of expenditure, are Salaries, Wages, Travel Expenses, Office Expenses, Payment for Professional and Special Services, Rents, Rates and Taxes/Royalty, Publications, Advertising, Sales and Publicity Expenses, etc. Although at one time, the objective was to limit the number of Detailed Heads, over the years these have multiplied in number.

3.10.1 Another important aspect of classification is allocation of expenditure between Capital and Revenues. Broadly defined, capital expenditure is incurred with the object of either increasing concrete assets of a material and permanent character or reducing recurring liabilities. As mentioned in Article 34 of the Audit Code, the following considerations are relevant in arriving at a decision whether or not expenditure is of capital nature.

"(a) It is not essential that the concrete assets should be productive in character or that they should even be revenue producing. A productive asset may be considered as one which produces sufficient revenue to afford a surplus over all charges relevant to its functioning. It may on rare occasions be necessary and justifiable to treat as capital a scheme not commercially remunerative but involving large expenditure, say for construction of a new city.

(b) The purpose of the commutation of recurring liabilities is their extinction or reduction. Although expenditure on this purpose may be genuinely capital expenditure, it is always necessary to examine from the point of view of economic financial administration whether such capital expenditure does not in fact merely replace one set of recurring payments by another, for example, whether the commutation by debit to capital of pension payments does not result in the substitution of equivalent payments of interest.

(c) It is inherent in the definition of capital expenditure that the assets produced should belong to the authority incurring the expenditure. Expenditure by Government on grants-in-aid to local bodies or institutions for the purpose of constructing assets which will belong to those local bodies or institutions cannot legitimately be considered as capital expenditure.

(d) Expenditure on a temporary asset cannot ordinarily be considered as expenditure of a capital nature."

3.10.2 Usually, capital bears all charges for the first construction of a project as well as charges for maintenance before it is opened for service. Capital receipts in so far as they relate to expenditure previously debited to capital accruing during the process of construction of a project should be utilized in reduction of expenditure already incurred.

3.10.3 Normally, capital expenditure is met from borrowed funds and other resources outside the revenue account. If, however, there is sufficient revenue surplus, it is open to Government to meet capital expenditure from its revenues. However, it is quite logical to utilise borrowed funds for meeting capital expenditure, as the liabilities in respect of borrowed funds are spread over a number of years; similarly, the benefits arising from the capital expenditure also flow over a period of years. Uniform principles should be followed in distinguishing capital expenditure from revenue expenditure, both in the Centre and the States, depending on the type of assets and their durability, because the distinction between capital expenditure and revenue expenditure is of crucial importance for the purpose of budgeting.

3.11 The main purpose of such elaborate classification is not only uniformity in accounting, as mentioned earlier, but also preparation of budget estimates under the prescribed heads of account. Besides, such classification of transactions subjects the concerned departmental officer to a periodical review in respect of the public receipts and payments in his charge, and ensures effective financial control and economy. In fact, classification of transactions is the most important tool for exercising control over public finance by the executive. Parliament/Legislature and Audit, as the classification indicates the nature of receipts and the purposes for which the monies have been spent. Only through the classified receipts and expenditure it is possible to ascertain whether the expected receipt have been collected and whether the monies have been spent for the purposes for which they were meant.

4

Control Over Public Finance

4.1 The following are the different stages for exercising control over public finance in India:

(i) Preparation of Budget.
(ii) Parliamentary/Legislative Approval of Budget.
(iii) Realization and Utilization of Funds According to the Approved Budget.
(iv) Scrutiny of Accounts by Audit Department and its Audit Reports on such Accounts.
(v) Parliamentary/Legislative Scrutiny of Public Finance Through the Public Accounts Committee and the Committee on Public Undertakings.

(i) PREPARATION OF BUDGET

5.1 The first stage of control over public finance is the control exercised by the executive Government through preparation of budget. The executive Government gives shape to its policy, plan, programme, etc. in preparing the annual budget.

5.2.1 In preparing the annual budget, the recommendations of the Finance Commission have a vital bearing for both the Union Government and the State Governments. According to the principles laid down by the Finance Commission, the Union Government determines shares of taxes and duties, which are to be paid to each State, after making an estimate of the total collection of the taxes and duties. The Union Government provides for the same in its budget as outgo from the Consolidated Fund of India. On the basis of the advance intimation received from the Union Government each State takes its share of the taxes and duties as its resources in preparing its budget, in the Union Budget the net amount available to Union Government, after deducting share of the States, is taken as receipt under the head "Taxes on Income other than Corporation Tax". In a State budget, its share in "Taxes on Income other than Corporation Tax" is shown as revenue receipt under the same head. On the other hand, the share of States in the "Union Excise Duties" is shown in the Union Budget as payment under the head "Grants-in-Aid and Contributions—Payment of States' share of Union Excise Duties". In a State Budget the corresponding receipt is shown under the head "Grams-in-Aid and Contributions—States' share of Union Excise Duties".

5.2.2 Similarly, the Union Government makes an estimate of the amount payable as grants-in-aid to States on the basis of the recommendations of the Finance Commission and makes provision for the same in its own budget. Each State also knows the amount of grants-in-aid from the Union Government to which it is eligible, for various purposes, on the basis of the recommendations of the Finance Commission and takes the same as its receipt in its own budget.

5.3 Role of the Planning Commission

5.3.1 The Finance Commission does one time job for five years. The Planning Commission has, however, an active role in each year in the preparation of the budget of the Union and the State Governments. At the time of considering the Annual Plan, the Planning Commission scrutinizes the position of resources of each year of the Union Government and the State Governments.

The Annual Plans are drawn up by the Union Government and each of the State Governments within the framework of the Five Year Plan approved by the National Development Council.

The Annual Plans are discussed by Planning Commission with the Union Government and each of the State Governments at two levels—(i) at the level of officials of the Planning Commission and the Government and (ii) at the Planning Commission level, when the discussions take place between the Union Minister concerned in the case of Union Government or the Chief Minister of a State with the Deputy Chairman of the Planning Commission.

5.3.2 At the official level, initially Adviser (Resources) of the Planning Commission holds discussions with the representatives of the Ministry of Finance for determining the availability of resources for the Annual Plan of the Union Government and the centrally sponsored schemes required to be implemented by the States, and also the likely contribution of the Union Government for the State Plans. In these discussions in the Planning Commission, representatives of various financial institutions like Life Insurance Corporation, Industrial Development Bank of India, etc., also remain present as they are expected to provide funds in the form of loans for certain specified objects, for example housing, development of small scale industries, etc.; these funds are taken as resources for the annual 'Plan'.

The position of resources is also discussed by the Adviser (Resources) of the Planning Commission with the Finance Secretary/Financial Commissioner of each State separately, keeping in view the non-plan commitments, and scope for mobilising additional resources, with a view to determine what should be the contribution of the State concerned towards its annual Plan and what will be the contribution of the Central Government. The representatives of the Ministry of Finance also take part in these discussions. These discussions are based on the projections of the State Government concerned, which are sent in advance to the Planning Commission. The minutes of these discussions are drawn up, after incorporating the changes in the projections of the State Government, as agreed to in these discussions. The minutes of the discussions indicate the resources which are expected to be available from different sources, estimated non-plan commitments, additional resources likely to be mobilised and the net resources that would be available for the annual 'Plan'. These agreed minutes are vital not only for finalising the annual 'Plan', but also preparation of the State budget.

5.3.3 At the second stage of official level discussions, technical experts of the Planning Commission in various fields headed by the respective Advisers discuss the Union Government's Annual Plan and the centrally sponsored schemes to be implemented by the States with the representatives of its Administrative Ministries. Thereafter, the technical experts headed by the respective Advisers of the Planning Commission discuss the Draft Annual Plan of each State with the officials of respective State Government for finalising its Annual Plan.

5.3.4 In the final round of discussions for finalisation of the

Annual Plan, the Ministers of the Union Government discuss the Central Annual Plan of their respective Ministries with the Planning Commission. In these final round of discussions in the Planning Commission, the Deputy Chairman of the Commission and his colleagues take part. In the case of the similar final round of discussions in the Planning Commission for finalising the Annual State Plans, the Chief Minister of each State takes part.

5.4.1 The budget provisions taken into account the Annual Plan thus finalised. The Union Government makes provision for its own Plan schemes and the centrally-sponsored schemes to be implemented by the States. The Union Budget also makes provision for the contributions of the Union Government for State Plans. On the other hand, each State makes provision for its own Plan schemes as also the centrally sponsored schemes. It also takes into account the contribution of the Union Government for its State plan in its own budget.

5.4.2 The limits for non-plan expenditure are also discussed at the time of discussion of resources for the Annual Plan. These limits are kept in view while framing the budget.

5.4.3 Besides, the estimates for borrowings of the Union Government (both internal and external borrowings) and of each State Government are taken into account at the time of discussions of resources for the Annual Plan. The internal borrowings include market loans, loans from various public sector financial institutions like Life Insurance Corporation of India, Industrial Development Bank of India, etc. The estimated borrowings are reflected in the Union budget as also the budget of each State. The repayment liabilities of earlier borrowings and interest thereon are also provided in the budget. The States take into account the concessions allowed by the Finance Commission in respect of their repayment liabilities in making budget provision.

5.4.4 In the resources discussions, the receipts from small savings schemes are taken into account. The States are entitled to a share of such receipts from small savings schemes, as long-term loans at concessional rate of interest. The Union budget provides for payment of such loan to States. Each State take into account such loan from the Union Government in its own budget.

5.5 It will be evident from the above narration how important are the recommendations of the Finance Commission and the decisions taken in the meetings in the Planning Commission for the preparation of the budgets of the Union Government and the State Governments.

6. Duties and Responsibilities or the Departmental Officers in Preparation of Budget

6.1 The process of preparation of budget starts at the lowest level of field office under a department. It moves upwards to the level of the Head of the Department, who is also the controlling officer for budgetary transactions. The departmental estimates then go from the Heads of the Departments to the administrative Ministry in the case of the Union Government and the administrative department of the Secretariat in the case of a State Government. Union Finance Ministry prepares the budget on the basis of budget estimates submitted by the administrative Ministries. In the case of a State, the Finance Department prepares the budget on the basis of the budget estimates sent by the administrative departments. The estimates are prepared separately for 'Plan' and 'Non-Plan' expenditures. Similarly, estimates are prepared separately for 'charged' and voted expenditure.

6.2 The process of preparing the budget estimates and the points to be taken into consideration in making such estimates are discussed below:

(i) The estimates for expenditure are based on an objective assessment of requirements, on the basis of the trends of actual expenditure in the past years, pace of actual expenditure during the current year, and also the estimated liabilities of the past, which would remain undischarged by the end of the current year.

(ii) The estimates for receipts are based on the latest trends and the decisions taken for raising additional resources. In preparing the estimates, the estimated amounts of receipts relating to earlier years which would remain unrealised till the end of the current year are also taken into account.

(iii) The estimating authorities have to remember that even the estimates for fixed establishments (standing or fixed charges) need to be reviewed from time to time for eliminating redundant expenditure in such establishments. Subject to this, the estimates for such fixed establishments vary from year to year due to normal growth of expenditure (for example, increment in pay, increase in dearness allowance, etc.), but the estimating authorities have no liberty to otherwise raise the estimates upwards.

(iv) (a) There is no definition in the Constitution of the expression 'New Service' used in Articles 115 and 205. Government of India had decided in consultation with the Comptroller and Auditor General of India that it would be better not to define this expression.

(b) The details in respect of any new service proposed to be included in the budget are required to be furnished in a prescribed form called "Memorandum for proposals involving expenditure on new service or new instrument of service".

(c) The provision for a new expenditure is not to be proposed in the estimates without acceptance by the Ministry of Finance in the case of Union Government or the Finance Department of the State concerned. In the Centre, approval of the Planning Commission is also obtained, whenever necessary, for such new expenditure. Similarly, in the case of a State, approval of the State Planning Board/State Planning Machinery is obtained, whenever necessary, for 'Plan' schemes. Before any such new expenditure is provided for in the budget for the first time, it is necessary to assess carefully, how many years it would continue, after taking into account all the difficulties that may be foreseen, for example, availability of required infrastructure, inputs, etc., so that no unnecessary provision is made. In the subsequent years also similar assessment is to be made in each year for limiting the provision in the budget which would be actually necessary in that year. This is a continuing process till completion of the item of work for which the provision is made.

(v) As mentioned in paragraph 20.1.7 of the book *Fundamentals of Government Budgeting in India* (Second Revised Edition, 1993), apart from the position of resources, the other points *inter alia* which are relevant for consideration for acceptance of a new item of expenditure for the budget are:

(1) whether the new item is intended to serve only a social objective or an economic objective or both social and economic objectives.

(2) whether the new item conforms to the objective of 'Plan' if it is a 'Plan' scheme, and, if so, whether its implementation is to be given priority over other items which can meet the same objective of the 'Plan'.

(3) whether this will generate productive employment, and, if so, the extent to which productive employment will be generated.

(4) its cost-benefit ratio, if it is intended to meet an economic objective.

(5) whether the objective of the proposed new scheme can be achieved a lower cost by augmenting any existing facility.

(6) whether the new scheme is technically feasible with indigenous inputs and resources.

(7) whether the proposal is most economic one or there are more economic alternatives available for consideration.

(8) whether the proposal involves any foreign exchange and, if so, to what extent and whether it will contribute to additional export or import substitution.

(9) whether any technical or financial collaboration is involved, and if so, the details thereof indicating whether credit facilities will be available from foreign suppliers/collaborators.

(10) whether the proposal involves any import of equipment or technology, and if so, whether the possibility of their availability indigenously has been explored.

(11) whether the proposal will in any way hinder the growth of indigenous entrepreneurship or production.

(12) whether the locational advantages/disadvantages have been examined, and if so, whether it will reduce or add to regional imbalances.

(vi) Any proposal for inclusion of capital expenditure and loans and advances in the budget should not exceed the limits prescribed by Finance Ministry in the case of Union Government or the Finance Department in the case of a State.

(vii) (a) As has been mentioned in paragraph 22.1.1 of the book *Fundamentals of Government Budgeting in India* (Second Revised Edition, 1993), accuracy is the *sine qua non* for making estimates for budget provision for any financial year. It is rather difficult, if not impossible, to prescribe how the desired accuracy can be achieved. Each estimating authority, however, has to bear in mind that in estimating the resources and their application one has to apply the wisdom which he would have applied in planning his own expenditure within his resources.

(b) As has been pointed out in paragraph 22.1.1 of the book *Fundamentals of Government Budgeting in India* (Second Revised Edition, 1993), "Overestimation of resources may result in undesirable tax concessions or provisions for avoidable expenditure. On the other hand, underestimation of resources may result in unnecessary tax burden or curtailment of high priority development expenditure. Similarly, overestimation of expenditure in some sector may result in unnecessary tax burden or exclusion of provision for some other high-priority development activity. Underestimation of expenditure on some items may also result in undesirable tax concessions or provision for items of lessor priority. Both overestimation of resources and underestimation of expenditure may ultimately result in unanticipated budget deficit or larger deficit than contemplated, with consequential adverse effect on economy of the country. Each estimating authority has, therefore, to keep these factors in mind while formulating its budget proposal."

(c) Departmental authorities should clearly understand that the final scrutiny by the Finance Ministry/Finance Department is no substitute for their own scrutiny, based on their administrative, professional, technical and grassroots experience. They have to remember that the scrutiny by the Finance Ministry/Finance Department is at a level, altogether different, and is really an overview based on its experience and specialisation gained over the years in examining similar or identical proposals from various other departments, keeping in view the overall economic position of the country/State as a whole.

(viii) Each Ministry/Department consolidates the figures by detailed heads of expenditure under the prescribed sub-heads, fixed by the Finance Ministry/Department, relating to each Major Head.

7. Role of the Ministry of Finance/Finance Department of a State in Preparation of Budget

Finance Ministry/Finance Department of a State has to finalise the budget on the basis of the estimates received from the various departments, keeping in view the following factors:

(i) Finance Ministry/Finance Department has to ensure that the estimates submitted by various departments conform to the guidelines issued by it, ceilings prescribed by it for loans and advances and other capital expenditure, final annual 'Plan', accepted recommendations of Finance Commission, etc.

(ii) Finance Ministry/Finance Department often imposes cuts in the estimates proposed by the various departments, keeping in view the overall resource position. Finance Ministry/Finance Department has, therefore, to guard against the possible temptation, which probably is very common, for the departments to prepare the estimates in such a manner that, they think, will be more readily acceptable, leading to inaccurate estimates in the shape of overestimation apprehending cuts by Finance Ministry/ Finance Department, or underestimation with the hope that the projected lower cost will be more acceptable to Finance Ministry/Finance Department.

(iii) Our need for developmental activities is much more than our available resources. It is, therefore, necessary to put the scarce resources to maximum use for quickest and maximum beneficial results in achieving certain social objective or economic objective or both. In issuing the guidelines to various estimating authorities, it is, therefore, very important for the Finance Ministry/Finance Department to lay down priorities for expenditure, particularly because of the prevalent regional imbalances in the level of development of different regions of the country/State. Besides, the cost of same type of development varies from place to place depending on the availability of inputs, weather conditions, communication facilities, etc. While, therefore, it may be necessary to take up some schemes for fulfilling the broad national objectives, there may be need for taking up other schemes to meet purely local needs. The criteria for determining priorities may, therefore, vary from place to place.

(iv) As mentioned in paragraphs 23.2 and 23.3 of the book *Fundamental of Government Budgeting in India* (Second Revised Edition, 1993) in formulating the tax proposals the Finance Ministry/Finance Department has to follow the following principles:

(a) "The aim of the welfare society should be to so regulate the taxation that the demand on an individual directly or indirectly is not beyond his capacity to contribute and is not oppressive. Any measure of taxation which does not take this elementary factor into consideration is unacceptable. The poor who constitute the majority in our country cannot be overburdened, when the major part of the fruits of development are enjoyed by cannot be overburdened, when the major part of the fruits of development are enjoyed by the minority affluent group while paying much less than what it should."

(b) "In formulating new tax proposals, therefore, the most important points which are to be taken into account are:

(i) what will be the effect of the proposal on the economy of the country/state; and

(ii) which sections of the people will be ultimately affected either directly or indirectly."

(c) "It has to be kept in mind that unthoughtful tax proposals may generate inflationary conditions leading to increased cost of development thus negating the very purpose for which additional resources are raised. Besides, in formulating new tax proposals the extent to which deficit financing will be resorted to has also to be kept in view. In a developing economy, deficit financing may have to be resorted to for planned development, but this has to be kept to the minimum by eliminating unproductive expenditure."

(v) Finance Ministry/Finance Department consolidates the detailed estimates received from each Ministry/ Department Major Headwise for receipts and net expenditure (*i.e.*, after deduction of estimated recoveries) for inclusion in the Annual Financial Statement (dealt with in details in the next section).

(vi) The effect of new tax proposals are included in the Annual Financial Statement and a Finance Bill (discussed in details in the next section) is also prepared for giving effect to the new tax proposals.

(vii) On the basis of detailed estimates received from the various Ministries/Departments, Finance Ministry/ Finance Department also prepares the 'Demands for Grants' and also 'Detailed Demands for Grants' discussed in details in the next section.

(ii)(a) PARLIAMENTARY/LEGISLATIVE APPROVAL OF BUDGET

The budget is not only an estimation of resources and their application for administrative purposes and welfare measures, but it is also an important tool for Government for implementation of its economic and social policies. As will be evident from the discussions which follows the Constitution has, however, given absolute power to the Parliament/State Legislature in this regard, as neither a *nayapaisa* can be withdrawn from the Consolidated Fund of India or the Consolidated Fund of a State nor a *nayapaisa* can be collected as additional tax or duty without the approval of the Parliament/State Legislative till the whole budgetary process is complete with the passing of the Appropriation Act and the Finance Act. Besides, as mentioned in paragraph 3.7 the Parliament/State Legislature may even prescribe the limits of borrowings and giving of guarantees by Government, although no such limit has yet been prescribed.

8. Annual Financial Statement

8.1 The Annual Financial Statement, which is the budget for a financial year is laid before the Parliament under Article 112 of the Constitution, which reads as follows:

"(1) The President shall in respect of every financial year cause to be laid before both the Houses of Parliament as statement of the estimated receipts and expenditure of the Government of India for that year, in this part referred to as the 'annual financial statement'.

(2) The estimates of expenditure embodied in the annual financial statement shall show separately:

(a) the sums required to meet expenditure described by this Constitution as expenditure charged upon the Consolidated Fund of India; and

(b) the sums required to meet other expenditure proposed to be made from the Consolidated Fund of India, and shall distinguish expenditure on revenue account from other expenditure.

(3) The following expenditure shall be expenditure charged on the Consolidated Fund of India:

(a) the emoluments and allowances of the President and other expenditure relating to his office;
(b) the salaries and allowances of the Chairman and Deputy Chairman of the Council of States and the Speaker and the Deputy Speaker of the House of the People;
(c) debt charges for which the Government of India is liable including interest, sinking fund charges and redemption charges, and other expenditure relating to the raising of loans and the service and redemption of debt;

(d) (i) the salaries, allowances and pensions payable to or in respect of judges of the Supreme Court;
(ii) the pensions payable to or in respect of judges of the Federal Court;
(iii) the pensions payable to or in respect of judges of any High Court which exercises jurisdiction in relation to any area included in the territory of India or which at any time before the commencement of this Constitution exercised jurisdiction in relation to any area included in a Governor's Province of the Dominion of India.

(e) the salary, allowances and pension payable to or in respect of the Comptroller and Auditor General of India;
(f) any sums required to satisfy any judgment; decree or award of any court or arbitral tribunal;
(g) any other expenditure declared by this Constitution or by Parliament by Law to be so charged."

8.2 Similarly, the Annual Financial Statement of a State is defined in Article 202, which reads as follows:

"(1) The Governor shall in respect of every financial year cause to be laid before the House or Houses of the Legislature of the State a statement of the estimated receipt and expenditure of the State for this year, in this part referred to as the 'Annual Finance Statement';

(2) The estimates of expenditure embodied in the annual financial statement shall show separately—

(a) the sums required to meet expenditure described by this Constitution as expenditure charged upon the Consolidated Fund of the State; and

(b) the sums required to meet other expenditure proposed to be made from the Consolidated Fund of the State;

and shall distinguish expenditure on revenue account from other expenditure.

(3) The following expenditure shall be expenditure charged on the Consolidated Fund of each State—

(a) the emoluments and allowances of the Governor and other expenditure relating to his office;

(b) the salaries and allowances of the Speaker and the Deputy Speaker of the Legislative Assembly and, in the case of a State having a Legislative Council, also of the Chairman and the Deputy Chairman of the Legislative Council;

(c) debt charges for which the State is liable including interest, sinking fund charges and redemption charges, and other expenditure relating to the raising of loans and the service and redemption of debt;

(d) expenditure in respect of salaries and allowances of judges of any High Court;

(e) any sums required to satisfy any judgment, decree or award of any court or arbitral tribunal;

(f) any other expenditure declared by the Constitution, or by the Legislature of the State by law, to be so charged."

8.3 Although Article 112 provides that the sums required to meet expenditure charged on the Consolidated Fund shall be shown separately from other expenditure proposed to be met from the Consolidated Fund, in the annual financial statement of the Central Government, the statements of proposed disbursements from the Consolidated Fund of India show the total figures of expenditure under each Major Head inclusive of expenditure to be charged on the Consolidated Fund of India. To meet the constitutional requirement mentioned above, a separate statement of disbursements proposed to be charged upon the Consolidated Fund of India is included in the annual financial statement showing such expenditure under each relevant Major Head. Incidentally, the form of the annual financial statement is prescribed by the Finance Ministry in the Centre. The form of the annual financial statement of a State is prescribed by its Financial Department, and more or less conforms to the form adopted in the Centre.

8.4.1 The following statements are included in the Annual Financial Statement of the Central Government for 1994-95, which also show the figures for 1992-93 (Accounts), 1993-94 (Budget), and 1993-94 (Revised):

(i) Statement I—Consolidated Fund of India which has the following divisions:

- (a) Revenue Account—Receipts
- (b) Revenue Account—Disbursements
- (c) Capital Account—Receipts
- (d) Capital Accounts—Disbursements.

(ii) Statement IA—Disbursement charged on the Consolidated Fund of India.

(iii) Statement II—Contingency Fund of India—Receipts and Disbursements.

(iv) Public Account of India:

- (a) Receipts,
- (b) Disbursements.

(v) Receipts and Expenditure of Union Territories without Legislature.

8.5.1 The contents of the statements mentioned above are discussed below:

8.5.2 Statement I— Consolidated Fund of India

(a) Revenue Account—Receipts

This statement contains the figures relating to (A) Tax Revenue, (B) Non-Tax Revenue, and (C) Grants-in-Aid and Contributions.

(1) Under A—Tax Revenue, the divisions are Taxes on Income and Expenditure, Taxes on Property and Capital Transactions, Taxes on Commodities and Services, and Taxes on Union Territories.

Taxes on Income and Expenditure include the figures of receipts under the Major Heads 0020 Corporation Tax, 0021 Taxes on Income other than Corporation Tax, 0023 Hotel Receipts Tax, 0024 Interest Tax and 0028 Other Taxes on Income and Expenditure.

Taxes on Property and Capital Transactions include Major Heads 0031 Estate Duty, 0032 Taxes on Wealth, 0033 Gift Tax.

Taxes on Commodities and Services are Major Heads 0037 Customs, 0038 Union Excise Duties, 0040 Sales Tax, 0045 Other Taxes and Duties on Commodities and Services.

Taxes of Union Territories show the Taxes of Delhi and other Union Territories.

(2) The divisions under B—Non-Tax Revenue are Fiscal Services, Interest Receipts, Dividends and Profits, Other Non-Tax Revenue.

Fiscal Services include 0046 Currency, Coinage and Mint and 0047 Other Fiscal Services.

Interest Receipts, Dividends and Profits include Major Heads 0049 Interest Receipts and 0050 Dividends and Profits.

Sub-divisions under 'Other Non-Tax Revenue' are General Services, Social and Community Services and Economic Services. General Services include Major Heads 0051 Public Service Commission, 0055 Police, 0057 Supplies and Disposals, 0058 Stationery and Printing, 0059 Public Works, 0070 Other Administrative Services, 0071 Contributions and Recoveries towards Pension and Other Retirement benefits, 0075 Miscellaneous General Services and 0076 Army, 0077 Navy, 0078 Air Force and 0079 Ordnance Factories of Defence Services, Social and Community Services include Major Heads 0202 Education,

Sports, Art and Culture, 0210 Medical and Public Health, 0211 Family Welfare, 0215 Water Supply and Sanitation, 0216 Housing, 0220 Information and Publicity, 0221 Broadcasting, 0230 Labour and Employment, 0235 Social Security and Welfare, 0250 Other Social Services, Economic Services include Major Heads 0401 Crop Husbandry, 0403 Animal Husbandry, 0404 Dairy Development, 0405 Fisheries, 0406 Forestry and Wild Life, 0408 Food Storage and Warehousing, 0435 Other Agricultural Programmes, 0701 Major and Medium Irrigation, 0702 Minor Irrigation, 0801 Power, 0802 Petroleum, 0810 Non-Conventional Sources of Energy, 0851 Village and Small Industries, 0852 Industries, 0853 Non-Ferrous Mining and Metallurgical Industries, 0875 Other Industries, 1051 Ports and Light Houses, 1052 Shipping, 1053 Civil Aviation, 1054 Roads and Bridges, 1275 Other Communication Services, 1401 Atomic Energy Research, 1425 Other Scientific Research, 1452 Tourism, 1453 Foreign Trade and Export Promotion, 1456 Civil Supplies, 1475 Other General Economic Services, 1201 Postal Receipts and 1225 Telecommunication Receipts. Railway Revenue as per Railway Budget is also included in 'Economic Services'.

(3) Grants-in-Aid and Contributions include the Major Heads 1605 External Grant Assistance; 1606 Aid Material and Equipment.

(4) As mentioned earlier, this statement also shows 'Non-Tax Revenue of Union Territories (Delhi and other Union Territories)'. Incidentally, Delhi ceased to be Union Territory in 1994-95 and there is no figure for Delhi for 1994-95.

(5) The totals of 'Tax-Revenue' and 'Non-Tax Revenue' are added to show 'Total Revenue Receipts'.

(6) This statement also shows 'Excess of disbursements under Revenue Account over Revenue Receipts', which is 'Revenue Deficit'.

(b) Revenue Account—Disbursements

The disbursements under 'Revenue Account' are shown under the divisions A—General Services, B—Social Services, C—Economic Services, and D—Grants-in-Aid and Contributions.

(1) 'General Services' include Organs of State, Fiscal Services, Interest Payment and Servicing in Debt, Administrative Services, Pensions and Miscellaneous General Services and Defence Services.

Organs of State include the Major Heads 2011 Parliament, 2012 President, Vice-President, etc. 2013 Council of Ministers, 2014 Administration of Justice, 2015 Elections and 2016 Audit.

The sub-divisions under Fiscal Services and Tax Collection and Other Fiscal Services. The Major Heads 2020 Collection of Taxes on Income and Expenditure, 2031 Collection of Estate Duty, Taxes on Wealth and Gift Tax, 2037 Customs, 2038 Union Excise Duties, 2045 Other Taxes and Duties on Commodities and Services are included under Fiscal Services. Other Fiscal Services include the Major Heads 2046 Currency, Coinage and Mint and 2047 Other Fiscal Services.

The Major Head 2049 Interest Payments falls under Interest Payment and Servicing of Debt.

Administrative Services include the Major Heads 2051 Public Service Commission, 2052 Secretariat-General Services, 2055 Police, 2056 Jails, 2057 Supplies and Disposals, 2058 Stationary and Printing, 2059 Public Works, 2061 External Affairs and 2070 Other Administrative Services.

Pensions and Miscellaneous General Services include the Major Heads 2071 Pensions and other Retirement Benefits and 2075 Miscellaneous General Services.

Defence Services include the Major Heads 2076 Defence Services—Army, 2077 Defence Services—Navy, 2078 Defence Services—Air Force and 2079 Defence Services—Ordnance Factories.

(2) B—Social Services include the Major Heads 2202 General Education, 2203 Technical Education, 2204 Sports and Youth Services, 2205 Art and Culture, 2210 Medical and Public Health, 2211 Family Welfare, 2215 Water Supply and Sanitation, 2216 Housing, 2217 Urban Development, 2220 Information and Publicity, 2221 Broadcasting, 2225 Welfare of Scheduled Castes, Scheduled Tribes and other Backward Classes, 2230 Labour and Employment, 2235 Social Security and Welfare, 2236 Nutrition, 2250 Other Social Services, 2251 Secretariat—Social Services.

(3) C—Economic Services has got Agriculture and Allied Activities, Rural Development, Special Areas Programmes, Irrigation and Flood Control, Energy, Industry and Minerals, Transport, Science Technology and Environment, General Economic Services, Grants-in-Aid and Coordination and Disbursements of Urban Territories as subdivisions.

Agriculture and Allied Activities include the Major Heads 2401 Crop Husbandry, 2402 Soil and Water Conservation, 2403 Animal Husbandry, 2404 Dairy Development, 2405 Fisheries, 2406 Forestry and Wild Life, 2407 Plantations, 2408 Food Storage and Warehousing, 2415 Agricultural Research and Education, 2416 Agricultural Financial Institutions, 2425 Cooperation and 2435 Other Agricultural Programmes.

The sub-division 'Rural Development' contains the Major Heads 2501 Special Programmes for Rural Development, 2505 Rural Employment, 2506 Law Reforms and 2515 Other Rural Development Programmes.

The Major Head 2552 North-Eastern Areas is under Special Areas Programmes.

The Major Heads 2701 Major and Medium Irrigation, 2702 Minor Irrigation, 2705 Common Areas Development, 2711 Flood Control and Drainage are included in the sub-division Irrigation and Flood Control.

The sub-division Energy contains the Major Heads 2801 Power, 2802 Petroleum, 2803 Coal and Lignite and 2810 Non-Conventional Sources of Energy.

The Major Heads 2851 Village and Small Industries, 2852 Industries, 2853 Non-ferrous Mining and Metallurgical Industries, 2875 Other Industries and 2885 Other Outlays on Industries and Minerals are under the sub-division Industry and Minerals.

The sub-division Transport contains the Major Heads 3051 Ports and Light Houses, 3052 Shipping, 3053 Civil Aviation, 3054 Roads and Bridges, 3055 Road Transport and 3056 Other Transport Services. Expenditure on Revenue Account as per Railway Budget is also included under this sub-division.

The Major Heads 3401 Atomic Energy Research, 3402 Space Research, 3403 Oceanographic Research, 3425 Other Scientific Research and 3435 Ecology and Environment are included under Science, Technology and Environment.

General Economic Services include the Major heads 3451 Secretariat—Economics Services, 3452 Tourism, 3453 Foreign Trade and Export Promotion, 3454 Census, Surveys and Statistics, 3455 Meteorology, 3456 Civil Supplies, 3465 General Financial and Trading Institutions, 3466 International Financial Institutions and 3475 Other General Economic Services.

The sub-division D Grants-in-Aid and Contributions includes the Major Heads 3601 Grants-in-Aid to State Governments, 3602 Grants-in-Aid to Union Territory Governments, 3603 Payment of States' Share of Union Excise Duties, 3605 Technical and Economic Cooperation with other countries and 3606 Aid Materials and Equipment.

Disbursements of Union Territories include disbursements on Revenue Account of Delhi and Other Union Territories. Delhi having ceased to be Union Territory in 1994-95, there is no figure for it for 1994-95.

The total of all the above is shown in this Statement as Total Revenue Disbursements.

Revenue Surplus

This Statement also shows 'Excess of Revenue over Disbursements', i.e., Revenue Surplus, if any. It may be mentioned here that since 1979-80 there has been no Revenue Surplus of the Central Government. At such, against the heading 'Excess of Revenue over Disbursements', there is no figure in this Statement of the Annual Finance Statement of the Central Government for 1994-95, which also shows the figures of 1992-93 (Accounts), 1993-94 (Budget), 1993-94 (Revised Estimate).

Revenue expenditure is the current (consumption) expenditure. Prudent financial policy requires that such expenditure should be fully met from revenue receipts. In fact, most sound financial policy would be to ensure that revenue receipts should not only meet revenue expenditure, but also leave a surplus to meet capital expenditure to the extent possible. On the other hand, when revenue expenditure exceeds revenue receipts, it means that consumption expenditure is being met from borrowed funds; such a position is unacceptable for any Government. Wiping out revenue deficit is, therefore, of prime importance for restoring health of Government finances. After having revenue deficits since 1979-80, Central Government has risen to the occasion, and got the "Fiscal Responsibility and Budget Management Bill" passed by the Lok Sabha aiming to eliminate revenue deficit by 2007-08.

(c) Capital Account—Receipts

The divisions under Capital Account—Receipts are A—Public Debt, B—Recoveries of Loans and Advances, and C—Other Receipts.

The Major Heads 6001 Internal Debt of Central Government and 6002 External Debt are under Public Debt. Internal Debt of Central Government consists of 91 Days Treasury Bills. Market Loans and Other Internal Debts of the Central Government.

The sub-division Recoveries of Loans and Advances shows such recoveries from State Governments, Union Territory Governments, Foreign Governments and such recoveries of Other Loans and Advances.

The Major Head 4000 Other Receipts is the only Major Head under the sub-division C—Other Receipts. This Statement shows the 'Total Capital Account Receipts'.

The total of Revenue Receipts is brought forward to this and the total of both is shown as 'Total—Consolidated Fund of India Receipts'.

(d) The Statement Capital Account—Disbursements

It includes the divisions Public Debt and Loans and Advances, in addition to those in the statement 'Revenue Account—Disbursements'. The nomenclatures of other divisions in the statement of Capital Account—Disbursements are almost similar to those in the statement of Revenue Account—Disbursement, except addition of the words 'Capital Account of' before each of the nomenclatures of divisions and sub-divisions. The nomenclatures of the Major Heads in this statement are also more or less similar to those in the statement for those in the Statement for Revenue Account—Disbursements, but the numerical codes of the Major Heads for Capital Account—Disbursements are different from those for Revenue Account—Disbursements. For example, against the Major Head 2210 Medical and Public Health in the Revenue Account, the Major Head in Capital Account is 4210 Medical and Public Health, which are similar except for the digit code. But against the Major Heads 2202 General Education. 2203 Technical Education and 2204 Sports and Youth Sciences, there is one Major Head 4202 Education, Sports, Art and Culture in the Capital Account.

The nomenclatures of the divisions under Loans and Advances are more or less similar lo those for capital expenditure, except that the word 'Loans' has been used instead of the words 'Capital Account of'. The numerical codes are also different for Major Heads. For example, as against the Major Head 4202 Education, Sports, Art and Culture in the case of capital disbursements, the Major Heads is 6202 Education, Sports, Art and Culture for Loans and Advances.

The totals of Capital Expenditure outside the Revenue Account, Public Debt and Loans and Advances have been added up in this Statement to show the 'Total—Capital Expenditure'. The 'Total—Consolidated Fund of India—Disbursements' shown in this statement has been arrived at after adding 'Total—Revenue Disbursements' with 'Total—Capital Expenditure'.

8.5.3 Statement 1A—Disbursements 'Charged' on the Consolidated Fund of India.

As mentioned earlier, the figures of disbursements 'charged' on the Consolidated Fund of India are included in the figures of the Statements 'Revenue Account—Disbursements' and 'Capital Account—Disbursements'. However, the Statement of Disbursements 'Charged' on the Consolidated Fund of India shows separately the figures of charged expenditure under each Major Head for meeting the Constitutional requirement under Article 112(2) of the Constitution, which requires that the expenditure 'charged' on the Consolidated Fund of India should be shown separately.

8.5.4 Statement II—Contingency Fund of India—Net exhibits the net transactions under the Major Heads 8000 Contingency Fund.

8.5.5 Statement III—Public Account of India includes the following:

(1) Public Account of India—Receipts
(2) Public Account of India— Disbursements

1. Public Account of India—Receipts is divided as,

(a) A—Small Savings, Provident Funds etc.
(b) B—Reserve Funds
(c) C— Deposits and Advances
(d) D—Suspense and Miscellaneous
(e) E—Remittances

A—Small Savings, Provident Fund, etc. include Small Savings, Provident Funds (State Provident Funds and Public Provident Funds) and Other Accounts (Postal Insurance and Life Annuity Fund and Other items).

B—Reserve Funds include Reserve Funds Bearing Interest (Railway Funds, Telecommunication Funds, Other Reserve Funds), Reserve Funds not bearing Interest (Central Road Fund, National Highways Permanent Bridges Fee Fund, Mines Welfare Funds, Sugar Development Fund, Railway Safety Works Fund and Other Reserve Funds).

C—Deposits and Advances include Deposits Bearing Interest (National Defence Fund, Family Pension-cum-Life Assurance Fund, etc., Other Deposits), Deposits not Bearing Interest (Civil Deposits, Deposits of Local Funds, Other Deposits) and Advances.

D—Suspense and Miscellaneous include Suspense Accounts (Net), Cheques and Bills (Net), Departmental Balances (Net), Cash Balance Investment and Others.

E—Remittances include Money Orders and Other Remittances.

Total of all the above heads in this Statement is shown as 'Total—Public Account Receipts'. After adding to this 'Total—Revenue Receipts' in Statement I and 'Total Capital Account Receipts' in Statement II the 'Grand Total' of all these receipts has been shown in this Statement. The 'Cash Balance' of the previous year has been added to the 'Grand Total' and shown as 'Total' receipts.

2. Public Account of India—Disbursements

This statement shows the figures of expenditure under the same heads as in the Statement of Public Account of India—Receipts.

The total of all the heads in this Statement is shown as 'Total—Public Account Disbursements'. After adding to this 'The Total Revenue Disbursements' in Statement I and 'Total—Capital Expenditure', in Statement II, the 'Grand Total' of payments has been shown in this Statement, 'Cash Balance' has been worked out and shown in this Statement after deducting the 'Grand Total' of payments from 'Grand Total' of receipts shown in the Statement of Public Account of India—Receipts.

8.5.6 Statement of Receipts and Expenditure of Union Territories shows the Receipts (Tax Revenue and Non-Tax Revenue) and Expenditure (Revenue Expenditure, Capital Expenditure and Loans and Advances) of the Union Territories without Legislature. It may be mentioned in this connection that Delhi ceased to be Union Territory in 1994-95 and hence there is no figure for Delhi for that year. In 1994-95, the Union Territories without Legislature were Andaman and Nicobar Islands, Dadar and Nagar Haveli, Lakshadweep, Chandigarh, and Daman and Diu.

9. As mentioned earlier, the Annual Financial Statement of a year shows the figures of the two earlier years (budget estimates and the revised estimates for the current year and the actual as per accounts for the previous year). One can, therefore, see the trends of receipts and expenditure in examining the figures of budget estimates for receipts and expenditure of a particular year, with reference to such figures for the earlier years. It has already been indicated earlier that the figures in the Annual Financial Statement are the net figures, i.e., net of refunds in the case of revenue receipts and recoveries in the case of figures of expenditure. Besides, the figures are by Major Heads only, which give an indication of the functions or services to which they relate. For proper understanding of the figures in the Annual Financial Statement, the Demands for Grants and the Finance Bill (described in the paragraphs following), a set of documents is laid before Parliament along with the Annual Financial Statement the Demands for Grants and the Finance Bill. This set of documents consists of (i) Key to Budget documents, (ii) Budget at a Glance, (iii) Receipts Budget, (iv) Expenditure Budget, Vol. I, (v) Expenditure Budget, Vol. II, and (vi) Memorandum Explaining the Provisions in the Finance Bill; all these documents will be described later on, indicating the contents of each and the particular use to which the same may be put.

10. Demands for Grants

10.1 Along with the Annual Financial Statement, Demands for Grants are also laid before Parliament. The Demands for Grants are laid before parliament under Article 113 of the Constitution, which reads as follows:

Procedure in Parliament with respect to estimates:

(1) So much of the estimates as relates to expenditure charged upon the Consolidated Fund of India shall not be submitted to the vote of Parliament, but nothing in this clause shall be construed as preventing the discussion in either House of Parliament of any of those estimates.

(2) So much of the said estimates as relates to other expenditure shall be submitted in the form of demands for grants to the House of the People, and the House of the People shall have power to assent, or to refuse to assent, to any demand, or to assent to any demand subject to a reduction of the amount specified therein.

(3) No demand for a grant shall be made except on the recommendation of the President.

10.2 The provisions for laying the Demands for Grants before a State Legislature are contained in Article 203 of the Constitution, which reads as follows:

(1) So much of the estimates as relates to expenditure charged upon the Consolidated Fund of a State shall not be submitted to the vote of the Legislative Assembly, but nothing in this clause shall be construed as preventing the discussion in the Legislature of any of those estimates.

(2) So much of the said estimates as relates to other expenditure shall be submitted in the form of demands for grants to the Legislative Assembly, and the Legislative Assembly shall have power to assent or refuse to assent to any demand, or to assent to any demand subject to a reduction of the amount specified therein.

(3) No demand for a grant shall be made except on the recommendations of the Governor.

10.3 The form of Demands for Grants is prescribed by the Ministry of Finance in the case of Central Government. Similarly, the form of Demands for Grants of a State is prescribed by its Finance Department. As against the net figures of expenditure (i.e., net expenditure after deduction of receipts and recoveries) by Major Heads shown in the Annual Financial Statement, the Demands for Grants show the gross figures of expenditure by Major Heads.

10.4 In the 'Introduction' to the Demands for Grants of Central Government for 1994-95 (excluding Railways) it has been explained that "Clause (2) of Article 113 of the Constitution requires that so much of the estimates of expenditure from the Consolidated Fund of India included in the Annual Financial Statement as are not 'charged' on the Fund shall be submitted in the form of Demands for Grants for the vote of the Lok Sabha. Normally one Demand is presented in respect of each Ministry/Department. In respect of some of the large Ministries/Departments, however, more than one Demand is presented. Each Demand normally includes the total provisions required for a Service, that is to say, expenditure on Revenue Account, as well as expenditure on Capital Account (including Loans) for the Service. Although the estimates of expenditure 'charged' on the Consolidated Fund of India are not required to be voted by Parliament, Clause (1) of Article 113 of the Constitution permits discussion thereon in either House of Parliament. Accordingly, a Demand for Grant also shows, distinctly in italics, the provision for expenditure, if any, 'charged' on the Consolidated Fund of India in relation to the Service represented by the Demand. Where the provision for a Service is entirely for expenditure 'charged' on the Consolidated Fund of India, for example, Interest Payments and Repayment of Debt, a separate Appropriation, as distinct from a Demand, is presented, although no vote is sought thereon."

10.5 In the Demands for Grants of Central Government (excluding Railways) for 1994-95 there are 98 Demands for Grants/ Appropriations. In addition, Delhi having become a National Capital Territory with effect from 1st December 1993, the book of Demands for Grants exhibits the estimates of transactions relating to Delhi for the period April 1993 to November 1993.

10.6 In the same Demand for Grant, there may be demands under several Major Heads. For example, in the Demand No. 1— Agriculture for 1994-95, the Major Heads are 2070 Other

Administrative Services, 2401 Crop Husbandry, 2435 Other Agricultural Programmes, 3451 Secretariat—Economic Services, 3601 Grants-in-Aid to State Governments, 3602 Grants-in-Aid to Union Territories Governments, 4401 Capital Outlay on Crop Husbandry, 7601 Loans and Advances to State Governments and 7602 Loans and Advances to Union Territories.

10.7 Again, the same Major Head may appear in several Demands for Grants. For example, the Major Head 3451 Secretariat—Economic Services appears in as many as 37 Demands for Grants for 1994-95, namely Demands No. 1 Agriculture, 3 Department of Agricultural Research and Education, 4 Department of Animal Husbandry and Dairying, 5 Department of Chemicals and Petrochemicals, 6 Department of Fertilizers, 7 Department of Civil Aviation, 8 Department of Tourism, 9 Ministry of Civil Supplies, Consumer Affairs and Public Distribution, 10 Ministry of Coal, 11 Department of Commerce, 13 Ministry of Communications, 23 Ministry of Environment and Forests, 38 Ministry of Food, 39 Ministry of Food Processing Industries, 51 Department of Industrial Development, 52 Development of Heavy Industry, 53 Development of Public Enterprises, 59 Department of Company Affairs, 60 Ministry of Mines, 61 Ministry of Non-Conventional Energy Sources, 64 Ministry of Petroleum and Natural Gas, 65 Planning, 66 Department of Statistics, 68 Ministry of Power, 69 Ministry of Rural Development, 70 Department of Wastelands Development, 71 Department of Science and Technology, 72 Department of Scientific and Industrial Research, 73 Department of Biotechnology, 74 Ministry of Steel, 75 Surface Transport, 78 Ministry of Textiles, 82 Ministry of Water Resources, 84 Atomic Energy, 86 Department of Electronics, 87 Department of Ocean Development, 88 Department of Space.

10.8 Thus it will appear that while the figure of expenditure under a Major Head is in one place in the Annual Financial Statement, the part of the same figure appear under several Demands for Grants. The reconciliation of the budget provisions by Major Heads of Accounts in the Annual Financial Statement with those in the Demands for Grants is shown in the Expenditure Budget, 1994-95, Volume I (one of the documents laid before Parliament with the Annual Financial Statement).

10.9 In a Demand for Grant, the figures of budget for the current year, revised estimate for the current year and the budget estimate for the ensuing year are shown. For example, in the Demands for Grants for 1994-95, the figures shows are for 1993-94 (Budget), 1993-94 (Revised) and 1994-95 Budget. The figures for Revenue expenditure are shown separately from those for Capital expenditure. Similarly, the total 'Charged' expenditure is shown separately from 'Voted' expenditure. Similarly, the 'Plan' expenditure is shown separately from 'Non-Plan' expenditure.

10.10 In a Demand for Grant, there are two parts. In the first part, the total estimate for 'Charged' and 'Voted' expenditure are shown separately for 'Revenue' and 'Capital' expenditure. In the second part the figures are shown by relevant Major Heads. In the Demands for Grants for 1994-95 the figures have been shown in the following manner:

I. Estimates of the amount required in the year ending 31st March 1995 to defray charges in respect of ...

Charged Voted	Revenue	Capital	Total (In crores of Rupees)

II. The Heads under which this Grant will be accounted for on behalf of the ...

Major Head	1993-94 Budget	1993-94 Revised	1994-95 Budget
Revenue Section			
Total Revenue Section			
Charged			
Voted			
Capital Section			
Charged			
Voted			

The *notes* added at the bottom, wherever necessary, are:

(1) The above estimates do not include the recoveries shown below which are adjusted in reduction of expenditure.
(2) The expenditure provisions, net of the above recoveries will be as under:

11. Detailed Demands for Grants

11.1 Subsequently, Detailed Demands for Grants are submitted to Parliament/State Legislature for each Demand for Grant, before it starts discussions on Demands for Grants. While a Demand for Grant shows the figures of estimates by Major Heads only, the Detailed Demand for Grants show the estimates up to detailed heads, i.e. standard objects for expenditure. For details of expenditure one has to necessarily consult the Detailed Demand for Grants.

11.2 Each Detailed Demand for Grants has got the following four parts:

(i) Part I—In this part, the service and the amount (gross) required for it during a financial year are shown in the same manner as in the case of Part I of the relevant Demand for Grant.
(ii) Part II—This part shows the distribution under various sub-heads (primary, i.e., basic units of appropriation) of the amount of the service shown in Part I. The break-up for 'Revenue' and 'Capital', 'Charged' and 'Voted', and 'Plan' and 'Non-Plan' are also shown, as in the case of Part II of a Demand for Grant, only difference being that the details up to sub-heads, i.e., primary units of appropriation are available in this part of Detailed Demand for Grant.
(iii) Part III—In this part, the provisions are shown by Detailed Heads (standard objects of expenditure) in respect of each sub-head, with similar break-up as in Part II.
(iv) Part IV—Estimated recoveries, if any, which are to be made in respect of estimated expenditure provided for in the Demand for Grants are shown in this part.

12. Finance Bill

The Finance Bill contains proposals for levy of new taxes and duties, modifications in existing taxes and duties and continuance of the existing taxes and duties without any modifications. The Finance Bill fulfils the requirements of Article 110(1)(a) of the Constitution in the case of Central Government and Article 199(1)(a) of the Constitution in the case of a State Government. A Finance Bill is a Money Bill under Article 110 of the Constitution in the case of the Central Government and Article 199 of the Constitution in the case of a State Government.

Introduction of a Finance Bill in the Parliament needs the recommendation of the President under Article 117 of the Constitution. Similarly, introduction of a Finance Bill in a State Legislature needs the recommendation of the Governor of the State, under Article 207 of the Constitution.

13.1 As mentioned in the key to the Budget documents for 1994-95, "The Budget documents presented, in terms of the Constitution have to fulfil certain legal and procedural requirements and hence may not by themselves give a clear indication of the major features of the Budget. To facilitate an easy comprehension of the Budget, certain explanatory documents are presented along with the Budget."

13.2 Key to the Budget Documents

Key to the Budget Documents explains in brief the cements of each of the other explanatory documents laid before Parliament along with the Annual Financial Statement. Demands for Grants and the Finance Bill.

13.3 Budget at a Glance

13.3.1 It has been stated in the Key to the budget documents for 1994-95 that "the Budget at a Glance shows in brief receipts and disbursements along with broad details of tax revenues and other receipts. This document also exhibits broad break-up of expenditure—Plan and non-Plan, allocation of Plan Outlays by sectors as well as by Ministries/Departments and details of resources transferred by the Central Government to State and Union Territory Governments. This document also shows the revenue deficit, the gross primary deficit, the budgetary deficit and the gross fiscal deficit of the Central Government."

In the explanatory note of the Budget at a Glance, it has been stated that the "Budget estimates are presented in this document in broad aggregates to facilitate easy understanding. For this purpose certain items of receipts and expenditures have been regrouped. For example, the expenditures of commercial departments have been taken net of their receipts so that increase in the volume of transactions does not inflate the figures on both sides. Similarly, short term loans and advances given to the States and recovered during the same year have been netted. Certain transactions which do not involve cash outgo, i.e., subscription to International Monetary Fund, investments in Nationalised banks, which are matched by receipts, have been excluded so that the focus is on real items of expenditure."

13.3.2 The expressions 'Revenue Deficit' and 'Revenue Surplus' have been explained earlier in paragraph 9.5.2 The expressions 'Budgetary Deficit', 'Fiscal Deficit' and 'Primary Deficit' used in the Budget at a Glance are explained below.

13.3.3 Budgetary Deficit

Budgetary Deficit is the excess of total expenditure (both revenue and capital) over total receipts (both revenue and capital). This gap is financed by the issue of 91-days Treasury Bills (these bills are mainly held by Reserve Bank of India), and draw down of cash balance. This is also called 'Overall Deficit'.

13.3.4 *Fiscal Deficit*

Fiscal Deficit is the difference between the revenue receipts plus certain non-debt capital receipts and the total expenditure including loans, net of repayments. This indicates the total borrowing requirements of Government from all sources.

13.3.5 Primary Deficit

Primary Deficit is measured by fiscal deficit less interest payments.

13.4 Receipts Budget

13.4.1 An analysis of the Figures of receipts is given in the Receipts Budget. As detailed below, the Receipts Budget gives details of revenue receipts and capital receipts, explains the estimates, shows the trends of receipts over the years and furnishers details of External assistance.

As stated in the introductory note in the Receipts Budget for 1994-95, it has got two Parts, namely, Part A—Revenue Receipts and Part B—Capital Receipts.

13.4.2 Part A explains the estimates of revenue receipts under two categories, namely, (a) Tax Revenue, and (b) Non-Tax Revenue for 1994-95 with reference to those for 1993-94 (Budget) and 1993-94 (Revised).

13.4.3 Part B deals with capital receipts including market loans, external assistance, small savings, Government provident funds, accretions to various deposit accounts, depreciation and reserve funds of departments like Railways, Telecommunications etc., for the year 1994-95 with reference to those for 1993-94 (Budget) and 1993-94 (Revised).

13.4.4 There are 12 annexures in the Receipts Budget for 1994-95 detailed below:

(i) Annexure 1 gives commodity-wise details of revenue from Custom Duties for the years 1992-93 (Actuals), 1993-94 (Budget), 1993-94 (Revised) and 1994-95 (Budget).

(ii) Annexure 2 gives commodity-wise details of revenues from Union Excise Duties for the years 1992-93 (Actuals), 1993-94 (Budget), 1993-94 (Revised) and 1994-95 (Budget).

(iii) Annexure 3 is the statement showing the State-wise percentage shares of Income-tax, Union Excise Duties and Grant in lieu of Railway Passenger Fares Tax under the recommendations of the Ninth Finance Commission (Second Report for 1990-91 to 1994-95).

(iv) Annexure 4 is the statement showing the State-wise distribution of Income-tax, Basic Excise Duties and Additional Excise Duties.

(v) Annexure 5 shows the financial results of the working of the Telecommunications Department for 1992-93 (Actuals), 1993-94 (Budget), 1993-94 (Revised) and 1994-95 (Budget), indicating the dividend to the general revenues.

(vi) Annexure 6 gives details of debt position, i.e. the outstanding internal and external debt and other liabilities of the Government of India at the end of 1993-94 (Revised Estimate) and 1994-95 (Budget Estimate). This Annexure includes the 'Statement of Liabilities' and the 'Statement of Assets' (capital investments and loans by the Central Government) at the end of 1950-51

(Actuals), 1989-90 (Actuals), 1990-91 (Actuals), 1991-92 (Actuals), 1992-93 (Actuals), 1993-94 (Revised) and 1994-95 (Budget).

(vii) Annexure 7 gives details of current rupee loans of the Central Government at the end of 1950-51 (Actuals), 1989-90 (Actuals), 1992-93 (Actuals), 1993-94 (Revised) and 1994-95 (Budget).

(viii) Annexure 8 indicates briefly the nature and magnitude of assistance in the form of loans, grants and commodities received from friendly foreign countries and International organizations giving the figures of estimates of receipts of external assistance and of repayments of principal and interest payments during the years 1993-94 (Budget and Revised) and 1994-95 (Budget).

This Annexure includes two statements. Statement 1 gives the estimates of receipts and repayments of 'External Loans' for 1993-94 (Budget), 1993-94 (Revised) and 1994-95 (Budget). Statement 2 gives the estimates of grants and commodity assistance from friendly foreign countries and international bodies for 1993-94 (Budget), 1993-94 (Revised) and 1994-95 (Budget).

(ix) Annexure 9 shows the trends of receipts (both revenue receipts and capital receipts) giving the figures of accounts (actuals) for 1985-86 to 1992-93, revised estimate for 1993-94 and budget estimate for 1994-95.

(x) Annexure 10 shows the trends of expenditure, under the headings 'Non-Plan expenditure' and 'Plan expenditure' with break-up of revenue expenditure and capital expenditure. The figures are actual for 1985-86 to 1992-93, revised estimate for 1993-94 and budget estimate for 1994-95.

(xi) Annexure 11 gives an analysis of Tax and Non-Tax revenue receipts included in Annexure 9.

(xii) Annexure 12 shows reconciliation between estimates of receipts shown in Annual Financial Statement (excluding the effect of budget proposals for 1994-95). The figures are for 1992-93 (Actuals), 1993-94 (Revised) and 1994-95 (Budget).

13.5 Expenditure Budget Vol. I

13.5.1 The introductory notes of the Expenditure Budget Vol. I for 1994-95 state that this document is intended to serve as the Explanatory Memorandum to the Budget of the Central Government in so far as the expenditure provisions are concerned. The introductory notes also explain that "the Expenditure provisions included in the various statements are net of recoveries, and receipts in the case of Commercial Undertakings, so as not to inflate the figures of expenditure/receipts.

13.5.2 Similarly, short-term loans and advances given to the States and recovered during the same year have also been netted. Certain transactions which do not involve a net cash outgo and are matched by receipts, for example, subscriptions to the International Monetary Fund, investment in share capital of Nationalised Banks etc., have also been netted, so as to focus attention on real items of expenditure.

13.5.3 The estimates of budgetary expenditure in this document exclude the transactions of Railways and Telecommunications except to the extent of Plan investments made from the General Budget. Incidentally, the Annual Financial Statement incorporates the expenditure of all the Central Government Ministries/Departments.

As mentioned earlier, the Demands for Grants are for gross amounts of expenditure without taking into account the recoveries taken in reduction of expenditure, while the figures in the Annual Financial Statement are net of these figures. Expenditure Budget Vol. I reconciles the figures of expenditure totals in the Annual Financial Statement and the Demands for Grants.

13.5.4 Expenditure Budget Vol. I for 1994-95 has got the following three parts, each consisting of several statements totalling 17. In addition, there are 7 Annexures.

(i) Part I General—contains Statements 1-3. This part also explains the variations in the revised estimate for 1993-94 with reference to budget estimates for the same year and also the variations in the budget estimates for 1994-95 with reference to revised estimate for 1993-94.

(ii) Part II Non-Plan Expenditure—contains Statements 4-11. It also indicates the important items of Non-Plan expenditure.

(iii) Part III Plan Outlay—contains Statement 12-17 and depicts the Plan outlay for various projects, programmes and schemes in 1994-95 included in the Central Plan.

13.5.5 The Statements and Annexures are briefly explained below:

(i) Statement 1 shows the summary of expenditure for 1993-94 (Budget), 1993-94 (Revised) and 1994-95 (Budget). The total expenditure has been shown in this statement with the totals of Non-Plan expenditure, Plan expenditure, Central assistance for State and Union Territory Plans, Budget support for Central Plan.

(ii) Statement 2 shows total expenditure by Ministries/ Departments with details of expenditure under Revenue and Capital as also Plan and Non-Plan for 1993-94 (Budget), 1993-94 (Revised) and 1994-95 (Budget).

(iii) Statement 3 shows the expenditure of Union Territories without Legislature with the same details as in Statement 2.

(iv) Statement 4 shows Non-Plan expenditure by broad categories, such as, 'Interest Payments', 'Defence', 'Subsidies', 'Postal Deficit', 'Exchange Loss under Foreign Currency Account', 'General Services', 'Social Services', 'Economic Services', 'Non-Plan Grants to States', 'Non-Plan Grants to Union Territory Governments', 'Grants to Foreign Governments', 'Non-Plan Capital Outlay', 'Non-Plan Loans to States', 'Non-Plan Loans to Union Territories', 'Non-Plan Loans to Public Enterprises', 'Loans to Foreign Governments', 'Other Non-Plan Loans', and 'Expenditure of Union Territories without Legislature' for 1993-94 (Budget), 1993-94 (Revised) and 1994-95 (Budget).

(v) Statement 5 shows the figures for subsidies for 1993-94 (Budget), 1993-94 (Revised) and 1994-95 (Budget).

(vi) Statement 6 shows the figures of subsidies excluding those for interest subsidies.

(vii) Statement 7 shows the figures for Departmental Commercial Undertakings for revenue expenditure, receipts and net expenditure for 1993-94 (Budget), 1993-94 (Revised) and 1994-95 (Budget).

(viii) Statement 8 shows the Non-Plan Capital outlay for 1993-94 (Budget), 1993-94 (Revised) and 1994-95 (Budget).

(ix) Statement 9 gives details of Non-Plan Loans to Public Enterprises for 1993-94 (Budget), 1993-94 (Revised) and 1994-95 (Budget).

(x) Statement 10 shows the figures of Non-Plan grants and loans to State and Union Territory Governments for 1993-94 (Budget), 1993-94 (Revised) and 1994-95 (Budget).

(xi) Statement 11 shows the figures grants and loans to foreign Governments for 1993-94 (Budget), 1993-94 (Revised) and 1994-95 (Budget).

(xii) Statement 12 shows the figures of Central Plan by Ministries/Departments for 1993-94 (Budget), 1993-94 (Revised) and 1994-95 (Budget).

(xiii) Statement 13 shows the Central Plan Outlay by Heads of Development for 1993-94 (Budget), 1993-94 (Revised) and 1994-95 (Budget).

(xiv) Statement 14 exhibits the Plan figures of investment in different Public Enterprises in the shape of equity and loans and their total for 1993-94 (Budget), 1993-94 (Revised) and 1994-95 (Budget).

(xv) Statement 15 shows the resources of individual public enterprises as per advised estimates for 1993-94 and budget estimate for 1994-95.

(xvi) Statement 16 shows the figures of Central assistance for State and Union Territory Plans for 1993-94 (Budget), 1993-94 (Revised) and 1994-95 (Budget).

(xvii) Statement 17 gives figures of Plan grants and loans to State and Union Territory Governments for 1993-94 (Budget), 1993-94 (Revised) and 1994-95 (Budget).

(xviii) Annexure 1—This shows the budget provisions by heads of accounts. The figures in this Annexure are the net figures. The figures are for 1993-94 (Budget), 1993-94 (Revised) and 1994-95 (Budget).

(xix) Annexure 2 reconciles the figures of expenditure shown in the Demands for Grants, Annual Financial Statement and Annexure 1.

(xx) Annexure 3 shows the trends of expenditure from 1985-86 onwards, with details of subsidies, other Non-Plan revenue expenditure and details of Plan expenditure. The figures for 1985-86 to 1992-93 are those of accounts. The figures of revised estimates for 1993-94 and budget estimates for 1994-95 have also been indicated.

(xxi) Annexure 4 shows the figures of contributions to International bodies for 1992-93 (Actuals), 1993-94 (Budget), 1993-94 (Revised) and 1994-95 (Budget).

(xxii) Annexure 5 gives the figures of guarantees given by the Central Government which were outstanding as on 31st March 1993.

(xxiii) Annexure 6 gives information of grant-in-aid exceeding Rs. 5 lakhs (recurring) of Rs. 10 lakhs (non-recurring) sanctioned to private institutions/organizations etc., during 1992-93.

(xxiv) Annexure 7 gives details of estimated strength of establishment and provision for each Ministry/ Department as on 1st March 1993, 1st March 1994 and 1st March 1995.

13.6 Expenditure Budget Vol. II

13.6.1 It has been stated in the Key to budget documents for 1994-95 that, "To understand the objectives underlying the expenditure proposed in the Demands for Grants a brief description of the various items of expenditure on major programmes included in the Demands together with the reasons for variation between the original budget and revised budget for the current year, and the requirements for the budget year are given in this volume."

13.6.2 Expenditure Budget Vol. II contains notes on various Demands for Grants for better appreciation of the Demands for Grants.

13.7 Memorandum Explaining the Provisions in the Finance Bill

13.7.1 As mentioned in the Key to the Budget Document, the Memorandum explaining the provisions in the Finance Bill facilities understanding of the taxation proposals made in the Finance Bill.

13.8.1 The descriptions of the above mentioned documents clearly indicate that adequate information and details are available in them for meaningful discussions of the budget in the Parliament.

13.8.2 Apart from the documents mentioned above, the following relevant documents are also available at the time of discussions of the budget proposals in the Parliament, and are expected to be useful to the Members of Parliament for participating effectively in the budget discussions.

13.8.3 *Economic Survey*

Economic Survey for the current year is prepared by the Ministry of Finance and laid before the Parliament a few days ahead of the date of presentation of the budget for the ensuing year. Detailed analysis of the economic situation of the country is available in the Economic Survey. This also includes analysis of the budgetary position of the Centre and States for the current year and a few past years indicating the revenue surplus/deficit, as also the overall surplus/deficit. The Economic Survey also gives detailed analysis of the trends in agriculture, industry, infrastructure, employment, money supply, imports, exports, prices, foreign exchange resources, balance of payments, etc. The Economic Survey facilitates appreciation of the resource position of the country, budget allocations and also the possible impact of the budget proposals of Government of the other sectors of economy.

13.8.4 *Performance Budget*

The budget of Government is a financial budget showing estimated resources (i.e., moneys) and their application for administration purposes and welfare measures. This financial budget does not indicate what on the ground is sought to be achieved by applying the resources.

After independence, naturally developmental activities gradually gained momentum. As mentioned in the book *Fundamentals of Government Budgeting in India* (paragraph 15), the "need for showing what on ground is sought to be achieved with reference to the money provided in the budget was being increasingly felt as the developmental activities were gradually gaining momentum. The idea was to ensure that value for the money was actually being obtained. This led to introduction of Performance

Budget in the Centre. The Performance Budgets set out what is sought to be achieved correlating them to the financial outlays, so that it can be found out whether the desired results have been obtained commensurate with the money actually spent."

Each Ministry/Department of the Central Government lays it before the Parliament prior to commencement of discussions of its Demands for Grants in the Parliament.

Many of the State Governments have also started submitting Performance Budgets of its various departments in their Legislatures.

13.8.5 *Annual Report*

Each Ministry/Department of the Central Government prepares a detailed report on its activities during the current year and submits it to the Parliament before discussions start on the budget for the ensuring year.

13.9 The documents mentioned below are also useful at the time of budget discussions.

(a) *Audit Reports of the Comptroller and Auditor General of India*

The Audit Reports of the Comptroller and Auditor General of India, submitted under Article 151 of the Constitution to the President for being laid before Parliament and to the Governor of a State for being laid before the State Legislature, contain his observations about accuracy in estimating the receipts and expenditure, performance in collection of receipts, efficiency in incurring expenditure for the purpose for which money was voted by Parliament/State Legislature, irregularities in collection of receipts and spending of money, impropriety in spending money, etc. In other words, an Audit Report gives an indication of how effective the Government has been in collecting the resources authorized by Parliament/State Legislature for collection and in applying the available resources for the purposes for which monies were voted by Parliament, pointing out to what extent policies, priorities, 'Plan' and projections adopted by Government in the past achieved the desired results.

(b) *Report on the Currency and Finance issued by the Reserve Bank of India*

This report is issued by the Reserve Bank of India, after the Central Budget and the State Budgets are laid before Parliament/State

Legislatures. The report contains *inter alia* two statements, one 'Budgetary position of the Government of India' and the other 'Consolidated Budgetary position of States', which show the revenue surplus/deficit and overall surplus/deficit of the Central Government and the State Governments respectively.

As mentioned in the book *Fundamentals of Government Budgeting in India* (Paragraph 9.5.2, Second Edition), this document gives a review of the economic situation of a particular year and an outlook for the next year along with detailed analysis of national income, saving and investment, agricultural and industrial outputs, price trends, monetary developments, banking developments, fiscal developments, foreign trade, balance of payments etc.

(c) Certain statutory bodies (for example, Life Insurance Corporation of India) set up by Government are not under the audit control of the Comptroller and Auditor General. The audit of accounts of such statutory bodies is conducted by the auditors appointed in the manner indicated in the legislations of the Central Government or the State Governments concerned which created these bodies. The annual accounts of such statutory bodies along with the Audit Reports thereon are submitted to the Parliament/State Legislatures concerned. These annual accounts and the Audit Reports on them are valuable documents in examining the budget proposals for the respective statutory bodies contained in the Central budget/State budgets concerned.

(d) Apart from his Audit Reports on the Central Government and State Governments, the Audit Reports of the Comptroller and Auditor General on the annual accounts of Government companies and corporations which are audited by him under Section 19 of the Comptroller and Auditor General's (Duties, Power and Conditions of Service) Act, 1971, are submitted to the Parliament/State Legislatures concerned along with their annual accounts under Section 19-A of the said Act. These annual accounts and the Audit Reports of the Comptroller and Auditor General enable the Parliament/State Legislatures concerned to examine critically the budget provisions for such Government companies and corporations contained in the Central budget or the State budget concerned.

14. Discussions on Budget

14.1 There are two stages of discussions of the budget for a year in the Parliament/State Legislature.

14.2 In the first stage, general discussions take place mainly based on the budget speech of the Finance Minister, which indicates the economic policies, taxation proposals, principles followed in allocation of resources, past performance and most importantly future projections. In other words, policies, priorities, plan and projections are covered in the general discussions.

14.3 In the second stage, the Demands for Grants are discussed in the Lok Sabha/State Legislative Assembly. The Detailed Demands for Grants are by then available and the discussions in this stage centre around the details available in the Detailed Demands for Grants.

14.4 As the discussions have to be completed within a time schedule, not all the Demands are ultimately discussed. Apart from general discussions on the Demands for Grants, mainly the discussions are based on the Cut Motions raised by the members of the opposition parties. As mentioned in the book *Fundamentals of Government Budgeting in India* (paragraph 13.8, Second Revised Edition), the 'Cut Motions' are for token cuts in the estimated provisions included in the Demands for Grants. When a member disapproves some provision, he moves such a motion, although only for a token reduction of provision. When the period fixed for discussions of 'Demands for Grants' is over, no further discussion is allowed by the Speaker, and the Demands for Grants which are not discussed are also taken as approved by the Lok Sabha/State Legislative Assembly. In Parliamentary parlance, the stoppage of discussions after the prescribed period is over is called application of guillotine by the Speaker. In this process many of the Demands for the Grants is get approved without any discussion in the Lok Sabha/State Legislature due to limitation of time at its disposal.

14.5 The ruling party or the group of parties (together with independent supporter, if any, is in majority in the Lok Sabha/State Legislature and, as such, the 'Cut Motions' moved by the opposition members get lost, and the Demand for Grants get approved by Parliament/State Legislative Assembly.

14.6 If, however, any 'Cut Motion' gels approved by the Lok Sabha/State Legislative Assembly, that will mean that the ruling party/group of parties has lost its majority and, in that event, the ruling Government resigns in deference to the sound Parliamentary principles and practice.

15. Vote on Account

15.1 Approval given by the Lok Sabha/State Legislative Assembly for the Demands for Grants does not by itself is any legal authority for withdrawals of funds from the Consolidated Fund of India/State. In other words, with Lok Sabha/State Legislative Assembly's approval of the Demands for Grants, Government is not in a position to incur any expenditure on the basis of the same, till the relevant Appropriation Bill becomes Appropriation Act, as discussed later, and the same gets approval of the President/State Governor.

15.2 As explained in paragraph 16 of the book *Fundamentals of Government Budgeting in India* (Second Revised Edition), usually, the budget for a financial year is presented to the Parliament/State Legislature towards the end of the preceding financial year. The whole process starting from presentation of the Annual Financial Statement to the Parliament/State Legislature, its consideration, voting of Demands for Grants, passing of the Appropriation Bills and their becoming law with the assent of the President/Governor takes some time, usually more than two months in the Centre. The new financial year starts in the meantime before the whole process is over. To enable the executive Government to incur expenditure during the intervening period, the Constitution provides for obtaining 'Vote on Account'. The clause (1) of Article 116 of the Constitution provides that the House of People shall have power to make any grant in advance in respect of the estimated expenditure for a part of the financial year, pending completion of the procedure prescribed in Article 113 of the Constitution for voting of grants for the entire financial year and passing of the relevant Appropriation Bill (Article 114 of the Constitution) authorising withdrawal of money from the Consolidated Fund of India against the grants for the entire financial year. These grants in advance are known as 'Vote on Account'.

15.3 Article 116(2) of the Constitution further provides that provisions of Articles 113 and 114 shall have effect in relation to the making of a grant under clause (1) of Article 116 and any law to be made under that clause as they have effect in relation to the making of a grant with regard to any expenditure mentioned in the Annual Financial Statement and the law to be made for the authorisation of appropriation of moneys out of the Consolidated Fund of India to meet such expenditure.

Similar provisions exist in Article 206 of the Constitution, for the States.

15.4 In other words, even for the amounts in 'Vote on Account', 'Demands for Grants' have to be approved by Parliament/State Legislature and its authorisation is to be obtained through Appropriation Bills for withdrawal of funds from the Consolidated Fund of India/the State; assent of the President/Governor is also to be obtained to the relevant Act for this purpose.

15.5 Thus the Central Government or a State Government is in a position to obtain 'Vote on Account' for one month or more, pending completion of the procedure prescribed by the Constitution for the 'Demands for Grants' and 'Appropriation Bills' for the entire financial year. The 'Vote on Account' being for very limited amounts and for limited periods, obtaining the same does not take much time.

16. Appropriation Bills

16.1 Article 114(3) of the Constitution provides that no money shall be withdrawn from the Consolidated Fund of India except under appropriation made by law passed by the Parliament in this regard. Similar provisions exist in Article 204(3) of the Constitution for incurring expenditure from the Consolidated Fund of a State only under appropriation made by State Legislature in this regard.

16.2 For withdrawal of funds from the Consolidated Fund of India on the basis of the Demands for Grants approved by the Lok Sabha and also the charged Appropriation, Appropriation Bills are introduced under Article 114 of the Constitution, which reads as follows:

(1) As soon as may be after the Grants under Article 113 have been made by the House of the People, there shall be introduced a Bill to provide for the appropriation out

of the Consolidated Fund of India of all moneys required to meet:

(a) the grants so made by the House of the People; and

(b) the expenditure charged on the Consolidated Fund of India but not exceeding in any case the amount shown in the statement previously laid before Parliament.

(2) No amendment shall be proposed to any such Bill in either House of Parliament which will have the effect of varying the amount or altering the destination of any grant so made or of varying the amount of any expenditure charged on the Consolidated Fund of India, and the decision of the person presiding as to whether an amendment is admissible under this clause shall be final.

(3) Subject to the provisions of Articles 115 and 116, no money shall be withdrawn from the Consolidated Fund of India except under appropriation made by law passed in accordance with the provisions of this article.

Similar provisions exist for the States in Article 204 of the Constitution for submission of Appropriation Bills before State Legislature.

16.3 According to Article 117(3) of the Constitution, recommendation of the President of India is necessary for introduction of Appropriation Bills in Parliament. Similarly, under Article 207(3), recommendation of the Governor of the State is necessary for introduction of Appropriation Bills in the State Legislature.

16.4 Under Article 110(1)(d) of the Constitution, an Appropriation Bill in the Centre is a Money Bill. Similarly, under Article 199(1)(d) of the Constitution an Appropriation Bill of a State is also a Money Bill.

The procedure for passing a Money Bill by the Parliament is contained in Article 109 of the Constitution. Similar provision for States is contained in Article 198 of the Constitution. In the Centre, the Money Bills are introduced in the Lok Sabha. In a State, the

Money Bills are introduced in the Legislative Assembly, even if it has a Legislative Council. The Rajya Sabha in the Centre and the Legislative Council in a State, if it has any, has to make its recommendations within fourteen days. If these recommendations are not accepted by the Lok Sabha (House of the People) or the Legislative Assembly, as the case may be, the recommendations have no effect. If the Rajya Sabha (Council of States) or the Legislative Council does not make any recommendation within fourteen days, the Money Bill is deemed to have been passed by both the Houses of Parliament/State Legislature.

The above-mentioned procedure is also followed in the case of an Appropriation Bill, as it is also a Money Bill.

16.5 In the Centre, an Appropriation Bill, passed by Parliament, becomes law, i.e., becomes Appropriation Act after assent of the President is obtained under Article 111 of the Constitution. Under Article 200 of the Constitution, an Appropriation Bill, passed by a State Legislature, becomes law after assent of the Governor is obtained.

16.6 Only after assent of the President/Governor is obtained to the relevant Appropriation Act, Government is in a position to draw fund against the Demands for Grants approved by the Lok Sabha/State Legislative Assembly.

17. Even for meeting unexpected demands on the resources, which cannot be stated in details or estimated precisely, or for meeting exceptional expenditure which does not form part of the current service of any financial year or for meeting additional demands arising in the course of the year for a service the budgeted funds for which prove inadequate approval of the Parliament/ State Legislature is necessary as discussed below:

(i) Vote of Credit

Under Article 116 of the Constitution the Lok Sabha (House of the People) is empowered to make a grant for meeting an unexpected demand upon the resources of India when on account of the magnitude or the indefinite character of the service the demand cannot be stated with the details ordinarily given in the Annual Financial Statement.

Similar provision exists in Article 206 of the Constitution empowering the State Legislature to make such a grant.

The above mentioned provisions in the Constitution enable the Central Government or a State Government to obtain a 'token grant' for a nominal amount for expenditure on a service, the exact extent or magnitude of which cannot be properly assessed and indicated immediately. The Government is then in a position to incur expenditure on the service till it is able to obtain supplementary grant at a subsequent stage for the entire expenditure after furnishing all necessary details.

(ii) Exceptional Grant

The Lok Sabha (House of the People) is also empowered under Article 116 of the Constitution to make an exceptional grant which forms no part of the current service of any financial year.

For the States, similar provisions exist in Article 206 of the Constitution.

(iii) Supplementary or Additional Grants

Under Article 115 of the Constitution, the Parliament has also power to grant, during the course of a financial year, additional amounts for expenditure on a service, the provision for which is found to be inadequate or for a new service not contemplated in the Annual Financial Statement. Such grant is called supplementary or additional grant.

For the State, the provisions for obtaining supplementary or additional grants are contained in Article 205 of the Constitution.

18. Excess Grant

Again at the end of each financial year, when the accounts of that year are finalised it is usually noticed that expenditure on certain services has exceeded the grant made by Parliament. Such excess expenditure is required to be regularised by obtaining excess grant from the Parliament under Article 115 of the Constitution.

Similar provision exists for States in Article 205 of the Constitution.

19. Control of Parliament over Public Finance is Absolute

From the narrations given above it will appear that the control of Parliament over Public Finance is absolute, not only in raising of resources, but also in determining the quantum and destination of such resources for application for the purpose of various services. Controls exercised by the executive Government over Public Finance is thus subordinate to the will and control of the Parliament.

(ii) (b) ESTIMATES COMMITTEE

The Estimates Committee is one of the three financial committees of the Parliament through which Parliamentary control over public finance is exercised. The other two committees are Public Accounts Committee and the Committee on Public undertakings discussed later in paragraphs 23.2 and 23.3.

20.1 As mentioned in paragraph 14.6, Lok Sabha does not usually have enough time to discuss in details all the Demands for Grants. When the time allotted for discussion of the Demands for Grants is over, all the Demands are taken as approved by Lok Sahha. As such, the Lok Sabha has set up a committee, which is called the Estimates Committee, to examine the details and the technical aspects of the estimates. The recommendations of the Estimates Committee have, however, prospective effect and does not have any effect on the budget under discussions in the Lok Sahha.

20.2 The Estimates Committee came into existence in April 1950 with 25 members elected by the Lok Sabha. Its strength was raised to 30 members from 1956-57. The Chairman of the Estimates Committee is appointed by the Speaker from amongst the members of the Committee. Apart from the functions generally performed by the Chairman of different Parliamentary Committees, the Chairman of the Estimates Committee performs certain other functions in relation to the working of the Committee. For example, the Chairman of the Estimates Committee decides, by convention, whether any information or document classified as secret should be called for from Government and even if the information or document is obtained whether the same should be made available to all the members. The Chairman of the Estimates Committee also decides whether cases regarding classification of 'charged' items should be examined by the Committee or not. Whenever necessary, the Chairman of the Estimates Committee also holds informal discussion with the Ministers or representatives of the Ministries.

Term of Office of the Estimates Committee

20.3 The term of one year of each Estimates Committee starts on 1st May every year. When a new Lok Sabha is formed the first Estimates Committee of that Lok Sabha may start functioning from any date following the date of constitution of the new Lok Sabha. The term of the Committee is, however, up to 30th April of the next year. The work of the Estimates Committee being of technical nature, a convention has been established so that as far as possible the same set of members remain in the Committee for two consecutive years.

20.4 Functions of the Estimates Committee

As mentioned in the book *Practice and Procedure of Parliament* (Kaul and Sakhder, Fourth Edition), the Estimates Committee "examines such of the estimates as may seem fit to it or are specifically referred to it by House or the Speaker, with a view:

— to report what economics, improvements in organization, efficiency or administrative reform, consistent with the policy underlying the estimates, may be effected;
— to suggest alternative policies in order to bring about efficiency and economy in administration;
— to examine whether the money is well laid out with the limits of the policy implied in the estimates; and
— to suggest the form in which the estimates shall be presented to Parliament."

It may be mentioned in the connection that while addressing the inaugural sitting of the Estimates Committee (1959-60), the then Speaker made the following observations about the exact scope of the function of the Estimates Committee:

> "Your function is not to lay down policy. Whatever policy is laid down by Parliament your business is to see that policy is carried out .... not divorced from its financial implications. It is only where a policy involves expenditure and you find that the policy has not worked properly, you are entitled and competent to go into it. Where the policy

is leading to waste, you are entitled to comment on it in a suitable way."

20.5 At the beginning of each of its term, the Estimates Committee selects the subjects relating to any part of the estimates relating to any Ministry or more for examining during the year ending 30th April following. The Committee does not usually take up the estimates relating to all the Ministries in one year. It selects the Ministries by rotation in such a manner that all the Ministries are covered during the life of each Lok Sabha.

The book *Practice and Procedure of Parliament* states that since 1960 the Estimates Committee has been selecting a few subjects in advance for examination by the Committee of the year, "Keeping in view that the subjects have not been examined by the Committee in the first round and that the subjects should be such as would entail the calling of considerable written information.

Ad hoc subjects of importance which *prima facie* appear to deserve examination in detail are also referred to the Committee from time to time by the Speaker of the House. Such references are made either through directions of the Speaker in the House or in the form of a communication to the Chairman of the Committee from the Speaker. The Committee may also take up any matter of sufficient importance for *ad hoc* examination by itself or on the suggestion of a member of the Committee provided that the matter does not relate to a proposal of Government which has not been finalized."

The Committee may call for details of expenditure 'charged' on the Consolidated Fund and examine whether the items of estimates have been correctly classified according to the Constitution and Acts of Parliament.

20.6 Whenever Government intends to introduce any change in the format of the budget or the information to be included in it, the proposed change is referred to the Estimates Committee for its recommendations.

If in the course of its working, the Estimates Committee comes across matters of special interest, it examined such matters if it considers necessary to bring them to the notice of Lok Sabha, even if the matters do not relate of particular estimate or estimates.

20.7 Examination by the Estimates Committee

Once the selection of subjects for examination is complete, the Estimates Committee calls for detailed information about the organization, set-up, activities, estimates, figures of actual expenditure etc., from the Ministry concerned in respect of each of the selected subjects.

It may be mentioned in this connection that the Estimates Committee appoints sub-committees headed by the respective convenors, "for securing flexibility in working and for detailed scrutiny of the subjects selected for examination." Each study group is allocated specific subjects for intensive study. The study groups are constituted by the Chairman of the Committee who selects the members of different study groups keeping in view their background, known aptitude and other factors. The experience gained by the members of the study groups enables them to specialize in particular subjects. This specialization of the members in different subjects facilitates examination of the officials of the Ministries on various relevant aspects. Apart from the selected subjects, the study groups are also allocated *ad hoc* subjects, special subjects, referred to the Committee, as also the reports on action taken by Government on earlier reports. The study group dealing with action taken by Government on earlier reports scrutinises the replies furnished by the Ministries, guide the Secretariat in drafting report on the replies furnished and discusses the draft reports before circulation to the main Committee. The study group dealing with procedural matters is composed of the convenors of all the study groups and is headed by the Chairman of the Committee. While on tour the Study Group may hold informal sittings but no decisions are taken at such sittings nor is any evidence taken.

The estimates Committee also undertakes study tours to acquaint itself with the working of the organisation under study at the field level. Usually the Committee divides itself into two zonal study groups.

On the basis of the information/details collected from the Ministries, as mentioned earlier, the members send their suggestions or points on which, they feel, further information is required. Thereafter, on the basis of all the details and information collected and suggestions of the members, a questionnaire is prepared. The questionnaire is considered by the sub-committee concerned and approval of the Chairman for it is obtained. The questionnaire is then sent to the Ministry concerned for furnishing replies.

According to the book *Practice and Procedure of Parliament*, "The fundamental objectives of examination by the Committee are economy and efficiency in administration and ensuring that money is well laid out within the limits of the policy implied in the estimates. The Committee does not go into or comment on a policy approved by Parliament but where it is established on evidence that a particular policy is not leading to the expected or desired results, or is leading to waste, it is the duty of the Committee to bring to the notice of the House that a change in the policy would be desirable.

The Committee is at liberty to examine policies laid down by Government as distinct from those approved by Parliament. It is also open to the Committee to examine any matter which may have been settled as a matter of policy by the Government in the discharge of its executive functions and the Committee has at times suggested alternative policies in order to bring about efficiency and economy in administration."

20.8 Evidence Taken by the Estimates Committee

In the course of its examination of the estimates of any Ministry/Department, the Estimates Committee calls officials concerned to give evidence before it. Usually the Secretary or the Head of the Department is expected to appear before the Committee for giving evidence. However, the Chairman may permit any other senior official to represent the Ministry/Department, if any request is made to him for that purpose. The Ministers are not called before the Committee. If necessary, the Chairman may have an informal discussion with the Minister concerned, but that too after the deliberations of the Committee are over. If considered necessary, the Committee may also invite non-officials, such as representatives of industries, experts, prominent public men, retired Government officers for giving evidence. Usually the selection of such non-official witnesses is made by the Committee taking into account the memoranda received from non-officials.

The Secretariat of the Committee prepares lists of points and/or questions for oral examination of the witnesses, incorporating therein suggestions, if any, received from the members of the Committee. Such a list of points and/or questions is circulated amongst members only after the same is approved by the Chairman. If any member wishes to ask a supplementary question, he may do so with the approval of the Chairman.

20.9 Minutes of the Meetings of the Estimates Committee

The minutes of the sittings of the Estimates Committee are recorded. These minutes of the sittings of the Committee are compiled separately for each report or Group of reports or ministry-wise, as is considered convenient. An authenticated copy of the minutes of the relevant sittings is laid on the Table of the House simultaneously with the report concerned.

20.10 Preparation of Report of the Estimates Committee

On completion of examination of the estimates of Ministry or a selected part thereof, the Secretariat of the Committee drafts a report, which is circulated to the members of the Committee after obtaining approval of the Chairman. A report of the Committee is considered and adopted in a sitting of the Committee.

If any part of a report of the sub-committee on Defence contains, in the opinion of the Chairman, any confidential matter, the same is not placed before the whole Committee. Such a portion of the report is forwarded by the Chairman to the Speaker. This procedure is also followed in the case of special and *ad hoc* reports on Defence containing confidential matter.

When it is not possible to get a report approved in a sitting of the Committee, the members of the Committee may authorise the Chairman to finalise the report by circulation. If any meeting of the Committee called for adopting a draft report is adjourned due to lack of quorum, the same is adopted by circulation.

The Committee sends advance copies of its reports, minus the recommendations, to the Ministries/Departments concerned for factual verification. These advance copies of reports are treated as 'Secret' till the reports are submitted to the House. When two or more Ministries/Departments are concerned, such a report is sent to the Department of Expenditure of the Ministry of Finance which acts as the coordinating agency. On receipt of the comments of the Ministries/Departments, amendments, if necessary, are carried out in the reports to make them factually correct before being presented to the Lok Sabha.

As a matter of convention, the reports of the Estimates Committee are not discussed in the House. The reasons for such a convention are mentioned in the book *'Practice and Procedure of Parliament'* as follows:

"As a convention, reports of the Committee, like those of the Public Accounts Committee, are not discussed by the House: the idea being that as the reports are detailed and deal with diverse subjects, recommendations of the Committee in general discussion may not be viewed in their proper perspective. The discussion may also not afford sufficient time and scope for presentation of full data which is a prerequisite for proper appreciation of the details of the reports.

Moreover, the discussion of the report in the House may proceed on party lines and thus come in the way of the healthy convention under which the Committee's recommendations are made without reference to party affiliations.

As far as the Government are concerned they are given full opportunity to present their point of view both at the time of factual verification of a draft report and again at the time of sending intimation regarding action taken on the recommendations of the Committee, and the Government's view point finds due place in the reports of the Committee.

It is open to the members to ask questions during Question Hour or raise points with regard to the implementation of the recommendations of the Committee when the demands for grants of the Ministry concerned are placed before the House."

20.11 Implementation of the Recommendations made by the Estimates Committee

After a report of the Estimates Committee is presented to the House, a copy of the same is sent to the Ministry concerned by the Secretariat. As a convention, Government generally accepts the recommendations of the Estimates Committee and acts upon them. The Ministry concerned is expected to send its replies to the recommendations of the Committee within six months from the date of presentation of the report before the House. On receipt of replies of Government on the recommendations of the Committee, these are examined by the study group for "Action Taken Reports". A draft report is then prepared by the study group containing further recommendations on the replies furnished by Government. After approval of the Chairman, the draft "Action Taken Report" is circulated amongst the members of the Committee for adoption. In certain cases such reports are also adopted in a sitting of the Committee. As in the case of the original report, factual verification of the report (excluding the recommendations) is got done by the Ministry before presentation to the House. The report is placed before the House after carrying out such amendments as may be necessary on the basis of the comments of the Ministry at the time of factual verification. Replies of Government on the recommendations of the Committee contained in the "Action Taken Report" are laid on the table of the House without further processing or comments by the Committee.

The Estimates Committee has a very useful role in making the Parliamentary/Legislative control over public finance comprehensive and effective. The accountability of the executive in respect of expenditure voted by Parliament/Legislature is secured through the Public Accounts Committee and the Committee on Public Undertakings. To make the Parliamentary control over public finance really comprehensive and effective, it is equally important that the estimates, which embody the policy of the Government, presented by the executive are subjected to a similar detailed scrutiny by a Parliamentary Committee; this role is performed by the Estimates Committee. This scrutiny by the Estimates Committee starts only after the budget is presented to Parliament/Legislature and its recommendations are only prospective without any effect on the budget under consideration of the Parliament. The recommendations of the Estimate Committee are expected to provide useful guidance for preparation of the estimates economically. Besides, the very fact that the estimates prepared by the Ministries/Departments would be subjected to detailed scrutiny by a Parliamentary Committee is expected to act as a deterrent to extravagance in making estimates.

(iii) REALISATION AND UTILISATION OF FUNDS ACCORDING TO THE APPROVED BUDGET

21.1 This is the second stage of executive control over public finance on the basis of budget approved by Parliament/State Legislature, i.e., after the passing of the Demand for Grants, Finance Act and Appropriation Act. The executive control at this stage is exercised through rules, regulations and procedures, framed by Government, in the main, for:

(i) Delegations of financial powers;
(ii) Collection of revenue/receipts and remission of dues;
(iii) Provision of funds;
(iv) Sanctioning of expenditure, remission of revenue, write-off of losses, etc.;
(v) Drawal and disbursement of funds and execution of contracts;
(vi) Maintenance of initial accounts including stores accounts;
(vii) Control over expenditure.

21.2 Delegation of Powers

21.2.1 As mentioned earlier, Government functions through delegation of powers to officials of different levels. Such delegation of financial powers is made in Central Government under a set of rules called Delegation of Financial Powers Rules, 1958, as amended from time to time. The financial powers of Government, which have not been delegated to any subordinate authority remain with the Finance Ministry/Finance Department.

21.2.2 Even if a financial power has been delegated by one superior authority to a subordinate authority, it shall be within the competence of the superior authority, if need be, to exercise that financial power delegated to a subordinate authority.

21.2.3 The General Financial Rules of the Central Government also provide that except in pursuance of the general delegation made by or with the approval of the President, a subordinate authority shall not, without the previous consent of the Finance Ministry, issue an order which:

(i) involves any grant of land, or assignment of revenue, or concession, grant, lease or licence of mineral or forest rights, or right to water power, any easement or privilege in respect of such concessions, or

(ii) involves relinquishment of revenue in anyway.

21.2.4 The delegated financial powers are to be exercised by a subordinate authority, subject to the conditions which are imposed by the authority which has delegated the powers.

21.2.5 The General Financial Rules of the Central Government provide that all departmental regulations in so far as they embody orders or instructions of a financial character, or have important financial bearing shall be made by, or with the approval of, the Finance Ministry.

21.3 Collection of Revenue/Receipts and Remission of Dues

The following are the more important rules and procedures prescribed in the General Financial Rules about collection of revenue/receipts and remission of dues:

(i) A controlling officer shall be responsible to ensure that all sums due to Government are regularly and promptly assessed, realized and duly credited to the Consolidated Fund or the Public Account.

(ii) The controlling officer shall arrange to obtain from his subordinate officers monthly accounts and returns in the suitable form claiming credit for the amounts paid into the treasury or otherwise accounted for, and compare them with the statements of treasury credits furnished by the Audit Officer or the Accounts Officer, as the case may be, to see that the amounts reported as collected have been duly credited to the Consolidated Fund or the Public Accounts. If in this process, wrong credits come to the notice of the controlling officer, he shall at once inform the Audit Officer or the Accounts Officer, as the case may be, with a view to the correction of the accounts. If any credits are claimed but not found in the accounts, enquiries shall be made first of the subordinate officer concerned.

(iii) The departmental accounts of revenue should be complied with reference to its own records and not from the returns prepared by the treasury. But the Treasury Officer may be required, when necessary, to verify the returns prepared for submission to the controlling officer.

(iv) Detailed rules and procedure regarding assessment, collection, allocation, remission and abandonment of revenue, shall be laid down in the regulations of the department responsible for the collection of revenue.

(v) In departments in which officers are required to receive moneys on behalf of Government and issue receipts therefor in the prescribed form, the departmental regulations should prescribe the procedural rules for the maintenance of a proper account of the receipt and issue of the receipt books, the number of receipt books to be issued at a time to each officer and a check with the officer's accounts of the used books when returned.

(vi) Amount due to Government shall not be left outstanding without sufficient reasons. Where such amounts appear to be irrecoverable, the orders of the competent authority shall be obtained for their adjustment.

(vii) Subject to any general or special orders issued by a Department of the Central Government, an Administrator or a Head of a Department responsible for the collection of revenue shall keep the Finance Ministry fully informed of the progress of collection of revenue under its control and of all important variations in such collections as compared with the budget estimates.

(viii) A claim to revenue shall not be remitted or abandoned save with the sanction of the competent authority.

21.4 Provision of Funds

21.4.1 As mentioned earlier (paragraph 16), the executive Government is not authorised to incur any expenditure in any financial year out of the Consolidated Fund in anticipation of the passing of the Appropriation Bill relating to the budget of that financial year, as the case may be.

21.4.2 The Finance Ministry/Department communicates to all the administrative Ministries/Departments, the Grants made by the Lok Sabha/State Legislative Assembly on the basis of the Demands for Grants placed before it and the Appropriations sanctioned by Parliament/State Legislature on the basis of the Appropriation Bill (Vote on Account) or the Appropriation Bill relating to the budget, as the case may be, passed by Parliament/State Legislative Assembly.

21.4.3 The administrative Ministry/Department or any other authority on whose behalf a Grant or Appropriation is authorised by Parliament/State Legislative Assembly, may distribute the sanctioned funds, where necessary, among the controlling officers and disbursing officers subordinate to it. Such distribution of sanctioned funds among the controlling officers and disbursing officers, in fact, indicates the consent of Government that those authorities should incur expenditure within the limits of the allotments placed at their disposal.

21.4.4 Subject to any special rules or orders issued by the President/Governor, (i) the whole or a part of the provisions under a primary unit as sanctioned may be placed at the disposal of a controlling or disbursing officer, or the primary unit may be broken into number of secondary units and the provision under any of these, wholly or in part, placed at his disposal, and (ii) a controlling officer at whose disposal an appropriation for a primary or secondary unit has been placed, may out of it allot funds for expenditure on a specific item or on a group of items.

21.4.5 A Grant or Appropriation is meant to cover the charges, including the liabilities if any of the past year, to be paid during the financial year or to be adjusted in the accounts of the financial year for which such Grant or Appropriation is sanctioned. Such charges can be authorised by competent authority, anytime before, but not after, the expiry of the financial year. Any unspent balance at the end of the financial year lapses and is not available for utilisation in the next year.

21.5 Sanctioning of Expenditure, Remission of Revenue, Write-off of Losses, etc.

A financial sanction is required to be issued, in the case of Central Government, by a competent authority strictly under the provisions of the Delegation of Financial Power Rules, 1958. (There are similar rules in the States.) Under the General Financial Rules of the Central Government, the financial sanctions are subject to, *inter alia*, the following general conditions:

(i) All sanctions to expenditure shall indicate the details of the provisions in the relevant grant or appropriation wherefrom expenditure is to be met.

(ii) All proposals for sanction to expenditure, including new expenditure, should indicate whether such expenditure can be met by valid appropriation or re-appropriation.

(iii) If it is essential to issue a sanction to expenditure before funds are communicated, the sanction should specify that such expenditure is subject to funds being communicated in the budget of the year.

(iv) A sanction comes into force from the date of issue unless any other date from which it shall come into force is specified therein.

(v) A sanction for any fresh charge shall, unless it is specifically renewed, lapse if no payment is made in whole or in part during a period of twelve months from the date of issue of the sanction. However, in the case of purchase of stores, a sanction will not lapse if the tender for supply has been accepted within the period of twelve months, even if no payment has been made in that period.

(vi) Copies of all financial sanctions and orders are to be sent to the Audit Officer and/or the Account Officer, as the case may be.

(vii) If any financial sanction requires the concurrence of the Finance Ministry, the same should be obtained and the fact that such concurrence has been obtained should be indicated in the sanction.

(viii) If a financial sanction or order is issued with the concurrence of the Comptroller and Auditor General of India, the fact should be mentioned therein.

(ix) All sanctions issued by the Finance Ministry should he endorsed to the Ministry of Home Affairs.

(x) Copies of all general financial orders issued by a Department of the Central Government should he supplied to the Comptroller and Auditor General.

(xi) All financial sanctions and orders involving payments from Government funds should be signed by the officers concerned in ink and should not be conveyed over cyclostyled signatures.

(xii) No authority should exercise its power of sanctioning expenditure to pass an order which will be directly or indirectly to its own advantage. Similarly, expenditure from public moneys should not be sanctioned for the benefit of a particular person or a section of the public, unless (1) a claim for the amount could he enforced in a court of law, or (2) the expenditure is in pursuance of a recognised policy or custom.

21.6 Drawal and Disbursement of Funds

21.6.1 There are very detailed rules for drawal and disbursement of Government funds both at the Centre and in the States, to ensure that drawal is made correctly, disbursement is made to the actual payee and there is no loss and fraud in drawing and disbursing Government funds.

21.6.2 A drawing officer is responsible for drawing a bill for the correct amount in the prescribed form after recording correct classification of expenditure. Bills should be drawn separately for 'charged' and 'voted' amounts. Except in the case of pay bills and the allowances drawn in pay bills, each other bill should indicate the progressive expenditure including the amount of the bill in which the entry is made. A drawing officer is also responsible for furnishing with a bill, copy of the sanction, where necessary, and the sub-vouchers (cash memo, etc.) and making necessary deductions (towards, GPF, income tax, recovery of over payment etc.). The encashment of a bill is watched through a Bill Register which *inter alia* indicates the date of presentation of the bill, token number given by the Treasury/Pay and Accounts Office, date of encashment, etc. A drawing officer or controlling officer who signs or countersigns a certificate for being attached to a bill shall be personally responsible for the facts certified to so far as it is his duty to know or the extent which he may reasonably be expected to be aware of them.

21.6.3 The Treasury/Pay and Accounts Office has to follow the prescribed rules and procedure so as to ensure that the bill has been drawn by an officer authorised to draw the same, it has been countersigned by the appropriate officer, if necessary, it is in prescribed form, it is arithmetically correct, the amount claimed is written both in figures and words and there are no erasures, besides ensuring that payment is made to the correct payee, who has been authorised to receive payment. The Treasury Officer/Pay and Accounts Officer passes a bill recording a payment order in writing on each bill presented for payment. He has to satisfy not only himself but also the Audit Officer that the claim is valid, and has further to prove that the payee has actually received the payment.

21.6.4 There are detailed rules for sale custody of cash drawn till payments are made to the correct payees against proper quittance. The Disbursing Officer is responsible for ensuring that these rules are scrupulously followed so that there is no loss of cash while in custody, payment is made to the correct payee, and no fraud takes place at the time of disbursement.

21.6.5 According to the General Financial Rules, no authority should incur any expenditure or enter into any liability involving expenditure or transfer moneys for investment or deposit from Government account unless such expenditure or transfer, as the case may be, has been sanctioned by general or special orders of Government or by any authority to which power has been duly delegated in this behalf. Besides, every officer incurring or authorising expenditure from public moneys should be guided by high standards of financial propriety. Every officer should also enforce financial order and strict economy at every step and see that all relevant financial rules and regulations are observed by his own office and by subordinate disbursing officers. Among the principles on which emphasis is generally laid are the following:

(i) Every officer is expected to exercise the same vigilance in respect of expenditure incurred from public moneys as a person of ordinary prudence would exercise in respect of expenditure of his own money.

(ii) The expenditure should not be *prima facie* more than the occasion demands.

21.6.6 The General Financial Rules provide that no contract shall be made by a subordinate authority which has not been directed or authorised to do so by or under the orders of the President/Governor. The President/Governor should be made a party to every contract of the Government and the words "for and on behalf of the President of India/Governor of the......" should follow the designation appended below the signature of the officer authorised in this behalf. The following general principles prescribed in the General Financial Rules arc to be observed by the subordinate authorities empowered to enter into contracts or agreements involving expenditure from public funds:

(i) The terms of a contract must be precise and definite and there must be no room for ambiguity or misconception therein.

(ii) Subject to adequate prior scrutiny of terms, general or special, if any, standard forms of contracts should he adopted, wherever possible. The alternatives used in the standard forms, which are not applicable, should be invariably scored out.

(iii) In cases where standard forms of contracts are not used, legal and financial advice should be taken in drafting the contracts and before they are finally entered into.

(iv) No relaxation of specifications agreed upon in contract or relaxation of the terms of an agreement entered into by Government should be made without proper examination of the financial effect involved in such relaxation. The interest of the public exchequer should be taken due care of before agreeing to any relaxation of agreement or contract.

(v) In selecting the tender to be accepted, the financial status of the individuals and firms tendering must be taken into consideration in addition to all other relevant factors. In the case of private individuals and firms tendering in foreign countries for contracts of large value, the Head of the Indian Mission concerned should be consulted.

(vi) Save in exceptional circumstances, no work of any kind should be commenced without prior execution of contract documents. Even in cases where a formal written contract is not made, no order for supplies, etc., should be placed without at least a written agreement as to the price.

(vii) Provision must be made in contracts for safeguarding Government property entrusted to a contractor and for recovery of hire charges, if any, therefor.

(viii) When a contract is likely to endure for a long period or where the contract provides for a clear schedule for the fulfilment of the various stages of the contract, it should include a provision for unconditional power of revocation or cancellation at the discretion of Government at any time on the expiry of reasonable notice to that effect. The period of notice should not normally be longer than 6 months.

All contracts should have a provision for recovery of liquidated damages for defaults on the part of the contractor, unless any special instructions are issued by the competent authority.

(ix) A cost plus contract should be avoided except where it is inevitable. (A cost plus contract means actual cost of service or supply plus profit at a fixed rate or percentage).

(x) The terms of contract for the purchase of perishable stores should invariably include a (separate) 'warranty clause'. In all contracts where a warranty clause is included, the position regarding delivery of goods at the ultimate destination free of cost in replacement of rejected ones should be made clear beyond doubt.

(xi) 'Lump sum' contracts should not be entered into except in cases of absolute necessity. Whenever such contracts are entered into, all possible safeguards to protect the interest of Government should invariably be provided for in the conditions of the contract.

(xii) A schedule of quantities with their issue rates of such materials, which are supplied departmentally, and are used in the contract work, should form an essential part of the contract.

(xiii) The question whether any sales tax, purchase tax, octroi, and terminal taxes and other local taxes and duties are to be paid and, if so, by which party, should be settled and cleared up before entering into any contract, involving transfer of movable property whatever its nature.

(xiv) Copies of all contracts and agreements above a prescribed financial limit should be sent to audit.

(xv) All contracts for purchase involving import of material from abroad should as a rule provide for purchases on f.o.b. basis and similarly, all sales contracts involving transport of material from India to other countries should be entered into on c.i.f. basis.

(xvi) The terms of a contract once entered into should not be materially varied without the previous consent of the authority competent to enter into the contract as so varied.

(xvii) No contract involving an uncertain or indefinite liability or any condition of an unusual character should be entered into without the previous consent of the Finance Ministry.

(xviii) Where escalation in respect of labour, overheads, customs duties, freight, etc., is provided for in a contract, the basis for the calculation of the same should be clearly indicated.

(xix) Generally contracts should be placed only after tenders have been invited openly. However, where open tenders are not invited and purchase is effected by negotiation or limited tenders the specific reasons for doing so should be recorded and approval of the competent authority taken in writing, unless such action is taken in accordance with any instructions issued by Government. Similarly, when lowest tender is not accepted, reasons should be recorded and approval obtained.

(xx) In the case of purchase of plant and machinery and equipment from foreign countries, whenever practicable and advantageous, contracts should be placed only after global tenders have been openly invited.

(xxi) No payments to contractors by way of compensation or otherwise, outside the strict terms of the contract or in excess of the contract rates may be authorised without the previous approval of the competent authority.

21.6.7 Finally, in the discharge of his ultimate responsibility for the administration of a grant or appropriation, or a part thereof, placed at his disposal, every controlling officer has to satisfy himself not only that adequate provisions exist within the departmental organisation for systematic internal checks to prevent and detect errors and irregularities in the financial proceedings of his subordinate officers and to guard against waste and loss of public money and stores, but also that the prescribed checks are effectively applied.

Under the General Financial Rules, provision that cannot be profitably utilised should not be spent hastily or in an ill-considered manner merely because it is available or that the lapse of a grant could be avoided. The existence of likely savings should not be seized as an opportunity for introducing fresh items of expenditure which might wait till the next year. Rush of expenditure in the closing months of the financial year shall be regarded as a breach of financial regularity and should be avoided.

21.7 Maintenance of Initial Accounts and Stores Accounts

21.7.1 The expression 'initial accounts' usually means the accounts which originate in a treasury or Pay and Accounts Office. But every drawing and disbursing officer also maintains accounts of amounts received by him and also the amounts drawn by him. The cash transactions are recorded in the cash book. Besides, registers are also maintained for various kinds of bills, like contingent bills, T.A. bills, medical bills, etc., through which the bills are passed and countersignature of controlling officer is obtained, whenever necessary, before a bill in appropriate form is drawn for presentation in the Treasury/Pay and Accounts Office. Before such a bill is presented to Treasury/Pay and Accounts Office, it is entered in the Bill Register, through which its encashment is watched. These accounts records enable the drawing and disbursing officers to keep watch over progress of expenditure against the allotments placed at their disposal, and submit expenditure statements to their controlling officers.

21.7.2 Similarly, each office is responsible for maintaining inventories of all fixtures, furnitures, stationery etc. In the cases of offices which handle stores (such as a Public Works Department office), a subordinate authority entrusted with stores of any kind shall maintain suitable accounts in respect of the stores in his charge with a view to preventing losses through theft, accident, fraud or otherwise and to making it possible at any time to check the actual balance with the book balance and the payment to suppliers etc.

21.7.3 Defence, Posts, Telegraphs and Railways have their own accounts organisations. Forest and Public Works Departments, which avail of the facility of drawals of fund by cheques from treasuries are responsible for maintaining and submitting their accounts according to the prescribed rules in this regard.

21.8 Control Over Expenditure

21.8.1 Under the General Financial Rules, each Department of the Central Government administratively concerned or the authority on whose behalf a Grant or Appropriation is authorised by Parliament shall be responsible for the control of expenditure against the sanctioned grants and appropriations placed at its disposal and shall exercise its control through the Heads of Departments and other controlling officers, if any, and Disbursing Officers subordinate to them. In order that the control of Departments over such expenditure may be effective and real and that the Controlling Officer should be in a position from month to month to estimate the likelihood of savings in and excesses over grants and appropriations, detailed procedure has been laid down in the General Financial Rules to be observed by all Departments and Controlling and Disbursing Officers subordinate to them, except where the Finance Ministry has agreed in writing to some other procedure.

21.8.2 For the purpose of control of expenditure, each Department of the Central Government should obtain, by the 15th of the following month, from the heads of departments and controlling officers under it the figures of expenditure of a month to enable it to watch the flow of expenditure against the sanctioned grant and appropriation for which it is accountable to Parliament.

21.8.3 For furnishing the figures of expenditure of a month, each controlling officer/head of department is required to maintain a register in prescribed form for each minor or sub-head of expenditure in which the details of expenditure are required to be recorded in respect to his own expenditure from portions of the grant or appropriation retained by him as also the expenditure incurred by each disbursing officer under him. Each disbursing officer maintains similar register of expenditure for reporting to the Controlling Officer/Head of Department the figures of expenditure of a month by the third day of the following month. If there are no entries in the register in any month, a *nil* statement is to be invariably sent.

21.8.4 Each controlling officer/head of department is required to maintain broadsheet for keeping watch on receipt of the expenditure statements from the disbursing officers subordinate to him.

21.8.5 A subordinate authority incurring expenditure is responsible for seeing that the allotment placed at its disposal is not exceeded and, where any excess over the allotment is apprehended, for obtaining additional allotment before incurring the excess expenditure.

21.8.6 On the basis of progress of expenditure from month to month, the Departments of the Central Government are able to surrender the savings in time or to obtain supplementary demands for likely excesses. The General Financial Rules provide that the savings should be surrendered to Government immediately after they are foreseen without waiting till the end of the year, unless they are required to meet excesses under some other unit or units which are definitely foreseen at the time.

(iv) SCRUTINY OF ACCOUNTS BY AUDIT DEPARTMENT AND ITS AUDIT REPORTS ON SUCH ACCOUNTS

22.1 In a parliamentary democracy Audit has an important role to play. As mentioned by Asok Chanda in his book *Indian Administration* (Second Edition), the accountability of the Executive to Parliament is absolute. The Executive handles the public finance. The Parliament secures the accountability of the Executive through the Audit Report of the Comptroller and Auditor General of India submitted to it through the President under Article 151(1) of the Constitution. Similarly, the Audit Reports of the Comptroller and Auditor General of India on the accounts of the States are submitted to the State Legislatures through the respective Governors, under Article 151(2) of the Constitution. It is said that the Comptroller and Auditor General is the "guide, philosopher and friend" of the Public Accounts Committee of the Parliament/State Legislature which considers the Report of the Comptroller and Auditor General of India, as a mini Parliament/State Legislature.

22.2.1 The Comptroller and Auditor General of India has been given necessary freedom under the Constitution so that he may discharge his duties without any fear and favour. It is up to him to decide what will be the contents of his Reports. On the other hand, it is for the Comptroller and Auditor General to maintain his dignity and independence, given by the Constitution, by his fair, impartial and detached outlook necessary for a dispassionate and objective assessment of the Executive's action in handling public finance. He has to ensure on behalf of the Parliament/State Legislature that any expenditure from Government funds conforms to "wisdom, faithfulness and economy" expected to be exercised by the Executive in handling public finance.

22.2.2 Independence of Audit is absolutely essential. Audit would not be in a position to discharge, without fear and favour, its duty of scrutinising the financial actions of various authorities, if it is dependent on one or more of such authorities whose actions or orders it may have to challenge. Besides, the power of Parliament and State Legislatures of voting money for expenditure given by the Constitution will he meaningless unless there is an independent and powerful Audit to bring to its notice the failure on the part of the executive in spending the money voted by it for the purpose for which it was voted and even if there is no change in destination of the voted money, failures to utilise the money efficiently, prudently and economically. An efficient Executive Government should also be proud of an independent Audit, which assists it in ensuring efficient financial administration through its subordinates by bringing to its notice lapses for timely action. As mentioned in the book *An Introduction to Indian Government Accounts and Audit* (Third Edition), "The true value of an Audit independent of the Executive is, therefore, to be gauged not by the irregularities which it actually discovers but by the certain effect of the knowledge that the auditor can and will, without fear or favour, report them if they come to his notice. That knowledge constitutes in itself the most effective security against irregularity." Full independence of Audit is adequately safeguarded under the Constitution.

22.3 It has been mentioned in the book *Indian Administration* (Second Edition) that "While the role assigned to the Comptroller and Auditor General in the Indian Constitution conforms to that in other parliamentary democracies, it is unfortunate that his relations with the Administration have tended to develop on somewhat unusual lines. In all recognized democracies, audit is not just tolerated as a necessary evil, but is looked upon as a valued ally which brings to notice procedural and technical irregularities and lapses on the part of individuals, whether they be errors of judgment, negligence, or acts and intents of dishonesty. The complementary roles of audit and administration are accepted as axiomatic, being essential for toning up the machinery of government. In the U.K., for instance, irregularities are rectified and disciplinary action initiated in the course of a current audit itself. The residue which finds its way into the Audit Report, relates, therefore, to major irregularities, uneconomic policies and procedures and improper exercise of discretion. The lapses of a department, as embodied in the Audit Reports, more particularly when endorsed by the Public Accounts Committee, are considered by the public as a virtual indictment of the department and of the individuals involved. This, in itself, acts as an effective deterrent in the commission of irregularities and secures their immediate rectification when they are brought to notice. Unfortunately, in India, this conception of complementary relationship has yet to be evolved. Audit continues to be considered as something alien, something extraneous and something of the nature of an impediment. A natural resistance has, thus, come to be developed in the administrative system to the absorption of the suggestions of Audit. This trend has become more and more pronounced in recent years." It is rather unfortunate that over the years since then there has been no improvement in the relation between the Audit and the Executive; rather they have drifted apart further. The Public Accounts Committee, however, continues to treat the Reports of the Comptroller and Auditor General with utmost importance.

22.4 According to the Audit Code, the functions of Audit are as follows:

(i) The primary function of Audit is to verify the accuracy and completeness of accounts to secure that all revenues and receipts collected are brought to account under the proper head, that all expenditure and disbursements are authorised, vouched, and correctly classified, and that the final account represents a complete and true statement of the financial transactions it purports to exhibit.

(ii) The right of independent criticism is inherent in the auditorial function and therefore the statutory provisions defining the position of the Comptroller and Auditor General and governing his functions explicitly or tacitly recognise his independence in the sphere of audit.

(iii) Government audit necessarily functions in a dual role, firstly on behalf of the Executive Government to check the compliance by Government servants subordinate to it, with the rules and orders issued by it in the discharge of its responsibility to the Legislature or other authority, and secondly, on behalf of the Legislature to secure that the Executive Government (aided by its subordinates) acts in accordance with the law and also with the views and requirements of the Legislature.

(iv) It is a first principle of Government audit to recognise the distinction between auditorial and administrative functions. It is a function of the Executive Government to make financial rules and orders and of the subordinates of the Executive Government to apply these rules and orders. It is the function of Audit to verify that financial rules and orders satisfy the provisions of the law and are otherwise free from audit objection, and that these rules and orders are properly applied. It is not otherwise the function of Audit to prescribe what such rules and orders shall be or to interfere with their administrative application.

(v) The audit of the Comptroller and Auditor General is a financial and not an administrative audit.

(vi) Criticism offered by the Indian Audit and Accounts Department must be limited to financial criticism based on the accounts. It is not the function of Audit to range over the field of administration or of statistics and offer suggestions how Government may better be conducted.

(vii) The Executive Government and not the Indian Audit and Accounts Department is responsible for enforcing economy in the expenditure of public moneys. It is, however, the duty of Audit to bring to notice wastefulness in public administration and infructuous expenditure, and in certain events, the criticism may be made public in the Audit Reports on the Appropriation Accounts. Generally a Government will welcome suggestions to promote economy based on information forthcoming from the accounts. Only the Accountant General should make such suggestions and the right to make them should be used with discrimination and sparingly. Suggestions of this kind should rarely be pressed after initial rejection by Government and rejection should not ordinarily form the subject of public comment.

(viii) In the course of scrutiny of accounts and transactions of Government, Audit is entitled to make such queries, and observations and to call for such vouchers, statements, returns and explanations in relation to them as it may consider necessary in the interest of proper discharge of its duties. All queries and observations shall be couched in language which is courteous and impersonal.

(ix) In auditing Government accounts Audit should not make independent enquiries from private individuals or members of the general public, as such action would amount to an encroachment on the functions of the Administration. Audit should confine itself to calling upon the Executive to furnish any necessary information and, in cases of difficulty, it should confer with the Executive as to the best means of obtaining the evidence which it requires.

(x) The final discretion whether an objection should be pressed or dropped rests with the auditor. Where a transaction requires the authorisation of a higher authority Audit must insist that such authorisation be obtained; or where a sum of money is recoverable Audit must insist on recovery save where authority to waive recovery has been delegated, or the competent authority has directed that recovery should be forgone. But all objections are not of equal importance and a residuary discretion rests with the Comptroller and Auditor

General and with the Accountant General under him to refrain from pressing an individual objection when there is sufficient assurance that the aim of audit to secure regularity and propriety, is safeguarded for the future.

22.5 The checks exercised by Audit in scrutinising various kinds of transactions, according to the provisions of the Audit Code, are discussed below:

(i) Audit of Receipts

The Audit of Receipts is regulated mainly with reference to the statutory provisions or financial rules or orders, as may be applicable. Generally speaking it is the responsibility of Audit to verify that the sums due are regularly recovered and checked against demand, and sums received are duly brought to in the accounts. In discharging these functions. Audit has to examine the correctness of the sums brought to account by the departmental authorities. Audit has to ascertain that adequate regulations and procedures exist in the department concerned to secure an effective check on the assessment, collection and accounting of the receipts and examine that such regulations and procedures are observed by the departmental authority. Audit has also to examine whether adequate internal checks exist against the commission of irregularities at the various stages of collection and accounting of receipts. When any scale or periodicity of recoveries of receipts has been prescribed, Audit has to examine whether the same has been followed. It is also incumbent on Audit to see that no amounts due to Government are left outstanding on its books without sufficient reason and that continuous action has been taken to recover the same. Amounts remaining outstanding should be carefully watched by Audit and whenever any dues appear to be irrecoverable, orders for their adjustment should be sought.

(ii) Audit of Expenditure

Audit has to see that the incurring of expenditure from the Consolidated Fund of India or the Consolidated Fund of a State is governed by the following essential conditions:

(a) that there should be provision of funds authorized by competent authority fixing the limits within which expenditure can be incurred;

(b) that the expenditure incurred should conform to the relevant provisions of Act, Constitution and of the laws made thereunder and should also be in accordance with the financial rules and regulations framed by competent authority; and

(c) that there should exist sanction, either special or general, accorded by competent authority, authorizing expenditure.

Audit examines whether expenditure has been incurred with due regard to broad and general principles of financial propriety and any case involving a breach of such principles resulting in improper expenditure or waste of public money is treated by Audit in the same manner as cases or irregular or unauthorized expenditure.

The other objects of audit of expenditure as set out in the Audit Code are to ensure:

(a) that the expenditure is incurred by an officer competent to incur it;

(b) that the claims are made in accordance with rules and are in proper form;

(c) that all prescribed preliminaries to expenditure are observed, such as proper estimates framed and approved by competent authority for works expenditure, a health certificate obtained, where necessary, before disbursement of pay to a Government servant, etc.;

(d) that the expenditure sanctioned for a limited period is not admitted in audit beyond that period without further sanction;

(e) that the rules regulating the method of payment have been duly observed by the disbursing officer;

(f) that payment has, as a fact, been made, and has been made to the proper person, and that it has been so acknowledged and recorded that a second claim against Government on the same account is impossible;

(g) that the charge is correctly classified, and that if a charge is debitable to the personal account of a contractor, employee or other individual or is recoverable from him under any rule or order, it is recorded as such in a prescribed account;

(h) that the rates paid for work done or supplies made are in accordance with any scale or schedule prescribed by competent authority;

(i) that the payments have been correctly brought to account in the original account; and

(j) that the general principles laid down in the General Financial Rules for entering into contracts (*vide* paragraph 22.6.6) are observed.

(iii) Audit Against Provisions of Funds

Audit against provision of funds is directed primarily to ascertaining that the money expended has been applied to the purpose or purposes for which the Grants and Appropriations have been intended to provide and that the amount of expenditure against each Grant or Appropriation does not exceed the amount provided in such Grant or Appropriation. Expenditure in excess of the amount of a Grant or Appropriation as well as expenditure not falling within the scope or intention of any Grant or Appropriation is treated by Audit as unauthorized expenditure. Although the responsibility for watching the progress of expenditure against a Grant or Appropriation devolves on the Executive, and the Executive is ultimately responsible for keeping the expenditure within the Grant or Appropriation, Audit renders all legitimate assistance to the Executive in this matter. Audit has to examine whether adequate and suitable arrangements exist in all departments of Government for the control of expenditure. Audit also scrutinizes the orders of allotment of funds and re-appropriations within Grants or Appropriations issued by the Executive authorities to see that these are covered by the relevant rules and procedures prescribed.

(iv) Audit of Sanctions to Expenditure

In addition to seeing that the expenditure is covered by a sanction, either general or special, Audit has to satisfy itself (1) that the sanction has been accorded by the authority competent to do so under the powers delegated to it in accordance with the provisions of the Constitution and of the Laws, Rules or Orders made thereunder or by the rules of delegation of financial authority made by competent authority, and (2) that the sanction is definite and there is no need for any reference to authority which has accorded the sanction or to any authority higher than the one which has accorded the sanction or to any authority higher than the one which has accorded the sanction. In the audit of sanctions to expenditure, the following guiding principles are observed by Audit:

(a) if the sanctioning authority is vested with full powers in respect of a certain class of expenditure, a sanction accorded under those powers can be challenged by Audit only on grounds of propriety;

(b) if it is vested with powers which may be exercised provided due regard is paid to certain criteria which are expressed in a general form, sanctions accorded under those powers can be challenged by Audit:

   (1) if the disregard of the criteria is considered to be so serious as to make the sanction perverse, or

   (2) if the facts of the case are such as to make the Audit confident that one or more of the criteria have been disregarded;

(c) if it is vested with powers which are expressed in precise terms, Audit is to ascertain that the order defining its powers is obeyed exactly in every instance;

(d) for the purpose of financial sanction a group of works which forms one project shall be considered as one work, and the necessity for obtaining the sanction of a higher authority to a project is not avoided by reason of the fact that the cost of each particular work in the project does not require such sanction;

(e) if anyone item of a scheme requires sanction of a higher authority, Audit should hold under objection any expenditure on that item until sanction to it is detained and in determining whether objection should be raised to expenditure on any other portion of the scheme prior to the receipt of such sanction it should be seen that the expenditure is not likely to exceed, at a latter date, the limit up to which sanction can be accorded by the original sanctioning authority;

(f) the sanctions with long period of currency and sanctions of permanent nature are reviewed periodically so that, if there is any reason to think that the Administrative authority concerned should be insisted to revise the sanction, such action is taken by Audit.

(v) Audit Against Regularity

The work of Audit against regularity is of great importance as it is of quasi-judicial nature. Examination of the rules and orders involves interpretation of the Constitution, statutes, rules and orders. But the final power of interpretation of rules and orders resides in the authority specified in the Constitution or the Authority which is the author of the rule or order so long as the interpretation is not against the orders of a Superior Authority or contrary to any established financial principle or rule. Interpretation by Audit is based on the plain meaning of the Article of the Constitution, Section of the Statute, rule or order, except where this is inconsistent with another Article, Section, rule or order; in such a case the inconsistent should be referred to the competent authority for resolution or removal. It is the duty of Audit to bring to the notice of the competent authority any expenditure which does not seem to be covered by the terms of the Article, Section, rule or order quoted as justifying it, and which has been incurred by placing upon the Article, Section, rule or order an interpretation which may seem to it not to be natural, plain or reasonable interpretation. In the case of regulations framed by a department of Government, Audit will accept what the department considers to be the correct interpretation of its own regulations, provided that such interpretation is not opposed to the ruling of any superior authority, or contrary to any established financial principle or rule. Such discretionary power of interpretation does not, however, give a department a free hand to interpret its rules to suit particular cases in other than a natural or reasonable manner. So long as a rule or regulation remains unamended the department is bound by it. Rules have to be carefully adhered to, and where in practice it is found that some discretion is necessary in the application of a rule, such discretion should be provided for in terms with respect to that rule. Audit has to see that the above procedure is followed by the departments of Government.

In conducting audit against regularity, Audit examines all financial rules and orders issued by Executive authorities, which affect expenditure and other transactions are examined by Audit to see that the rules, etc., are themselves *intra vires* and that the audit of transactions which they govern by may be efficiently conducted against them. In the scrutiny of rules and orders Audit has to see:

(a) that they are not inconsistent with any provisions of the Constitution or of any laws made thereunder;
(b) that they are consistent with the essential requirements of audit and accounts as determined by the Comptroller and Auditor General;
(c) that they do not conflict with the orders of, or rules made by, any higher authority;
(d) that, in case they have not been separately approved by competent authority, the issuing authority possesses the necessary rule-making power;
(e) that all orders of delegation of financial authority are properly examined and are acceptable in audit as, once such orders are accepted, audit of sanctions as well as of expenditure or other transactions may be conducted against them for any indefinite length of time.

There may be cases in which no objection can be raised in terms of an order of delegation, or other financial rule, yet Audit may feel that the order is likely to impair seriously the efficiency of financial control. If any such objection considered important, the same should be brought to the notice of the Finance Ministry or Department, for misusing the order.

(vi) Audit Against Propriety

All cases of irregularity are brought to light by Audit. However, there may be cases which may apparently conform to rules and orders, but involve improper expenditure or waste of public money. It is essential for Audit to bring to light such improper expenditure or waste of public money, which does not conform to the broad principles of orthodox finance, even if there is no irregularity as such. There are no precise rules for conducting audit against propriety. The purpose of audit against propriety is to sustain a reasonably high standard of public financial morality, of sound financial administration, and devotion to the financial interests of Government. In performing its duties, Audit has to follow the general principles mentioned below which have for long been recognized as standards of financial propriety:

(a) The expenditure should not be *prima facie* more than the occasion demands. Every public officer is expected to exercise the same vigilance in respect of expenditure incurred from public moneys as a person of ordinary prudence would exercise in respect of expenditure of his own money.

(b) No authority should exercise its powers of sanctioning expenditure to pass an order which will be directly or indirectly to its own advantage.

(c) Public moneys should not be utilized for the benefit of a particular person or section of the community unless:

   (i) the amount of expenditure involved is insignificant; or

   (ii) a claim for the amount could be enforced in a court of law; or

   (iii) the expenditure is in pursuance of a recognized policy or custom.

(d) The amount of allowances, such as travelling allowances, granted to meet expenditure of a particular type, should be so regulated that the allowances are not on the whole a source of profit to the recipients.

Audit against propriety is a delicate matter and requires much discretion and tact. Any expenditure considered improper should be expressed as violative of universally accepted standard of official conduct or financial administration and not as based upon 'Canons of Financial Propriety'.

(vii) Efficiency-cum-Performance Audit

It has already been mentioned in paragraph 13.8.4 that the Central Government and some of the State Governments prepare Performance Budgets setting out what is sought to be achieved correlating them to the financial outlays, so that it may be found out whether the desired results have been obtained commensurate with the money actually spent. In view of the ever increasing development activities and the huge amounts provided in the budget for the same, Audit has a very significant role in seeing that the value for the money spent has been really achieved. The work of audit in this direction is efficiency-cum-performance audit. As mentioned in paragraph 255-A of the book *An Introduction to Indian Government Accounts and Audit* (Third Edition, 1963), the objects of efficiency-cum-performance audit are to ascertain: (a) whether the various schemes are being run economically, and (b) whether they are actually yielding the results expected of them. As regards (a), the examination by Audit includes such aspects as failure to adhere to estimate due to inefficient handling or the lack of foresight etc., expensive delays, wasteful expenditure through lack of co-ordination, infructuous expenditure, losses, etc. As regards (b), it has to be ascertained how far the physical targets, returns or final objects of the scheme have been achieved.

22.6 In the offices of the Accountants General which maintain accounts of the State Governments, audit is conducted both centrally in the respective offices with reference to the vouchers/challans received with the Treasury Accounts and also locally with reference to the initial records maintained in various offices of State Governments. In the Centre, accounts of the Central Government are no longer maintained by the Audit Department, consequent on separation of accounts from audit. As such, the transactions of the Central Government are audited only locally in the various offices of the Central Government.

22.7 Audit conducted by the Indian Audit and Accounts Department is a test audit on selective basis. As such, all the individual transactions do not come under audit scrutiny.

Objections and observations in relation to any accounts or transactions are communicated initially to the disbursing officers. Sometimes such objections and observations are also intimated to the controlling officers simultaneously. More important objections and observations of Audit are brought to the notice of Government also. Audit pursues the objections and observations till these are settled to the reasonable satisfaction of Audit. As mentioned in the Audit Code, "An intelligent, prompt and vigorous pursuance of objections and early report of any important irregularity to Government are essential so that the Audit Reports required to be submitted by the Comptroller and Auditor General may have their full value." The disbursing officers, controlling officers and Government are primarily responsible for removal of objection and settlement of other points raised in audit. It is to the advantage of the disbursing officers and other departmental officers to rectify the irregularities pointed out by Audit at the earliest, as Audit does not pursue further the audit queries when the irregularities are rectified to the reasonable satisfaction of Audit. Unfortunately, this does not normally happen. A tendency has developed in the Executive to keep the audit queries pending for long or to circumvent the real issues by evasive replies. There are cases when defence is attempted in indefensible cases. As a result, those who are responsible for the omissions and commissions remain unaffected. Over the years, therefore an attitude of 'nothing happens' has developed in the lower echelons of the Administration towards the audit observations. Continuance of such an attitude will greatly affect the financial administration of the country in the long run. It is high time for the Executive to change its attitude towards Audit. On the other hand, pursuance of Audit observations should be really objective and cover essentials, having the non-essentials of trivial nature to be sorted out by the Executive, in such matters Audit would have done its part by bringing the cases to the notice of the Executive. But the Executive will have to be alert and responsive on these apparent trivial audit observations, as persistence of such cases ultimately affects the financial administration irreparably.

22.8.1 In the case of the Union Government, the Comptroller and Auditor General submits the following Audit Reports for being laid before Parliament:

(i) Audit Report (Civil)
(ii) Audit Report (Revenue Receipts)
(iii) Audit Report (Railways)
(iv) Audit Report (Posts & Telegraphs)
(v) Audit Report (Defence Services)
(vi) Audit Report (Commercial)

In the cases of the States, apart from the Audit Report (Civil), separate Audit Reports, such as Audit Report (Revenue Receipt) and Audit Report (Commercial) are also submitted. For smaller States, a single Audit Report may also include observations relating to revenue receipts, State commercial undertakings, etc.

22.8.2 As mentioned in the Audit Code the following general limitations are observed in selecting subjects for comment in an Audit Report:

(a) Comments are confined to such matters as should be of real and practical concern to the Parliament/State Legislature. Individual cases are not mentioned unless they are really important as involving serious transgression of statutory provisions, rules or orders leading, or likely to lead, to loss of public money or serious breaches of audit procedure or audit safeguards. Petty cases are, however, mentioned if minor irregularities of one class are so numerous as to produce an appreciable cumulative effect. There is no need to mention an irregularity which has been completely rectified, unless there is a substantial point to be made.

(b) Cases which are subjudice will not be mentioned in such a way as to prejudice the claim or defence in court. This rule applies to cases actually decided in a lower court until such time as the department concerned intimates that the litigation is finally concluded.

(c) It is important that all details necessary for understanding an irregularity are furnished and the same is described in plain language, so that even a person not versed with the rules, procedures and accounts may understand its bearing on the financial interests of Government. Technical expressions are seldom used; and, when their use is unavoidable, they are explained.

(d) Any irregularity reported in an Audit Report briefly contains the following information:

(i) an explanation of the transaction;
(ii) a description of the nature and magnitude of the irregularity;
(iii) any extenuating circumstances that may exist;
(iv) any defect in system which led up to the irregularity;
(v) the remedial or preventive measures adopted; and
(vi) the adequacy of those measures.

22.8.3 According to the guidelines given in the Audit Code "Audit Report should be self-contained in respect of all matters with which it deals. It is essential that a detached, dispassionate and technical attitude should be maintained and that expressions suggesting a political opinion or bias should be avoided. The report should be so designed as to serve a double purpose. To the Government concerned, the report will show the extent to which its subordinates are complying with its rules and orders, and will often suggest directions in which those rules and orders can with advantage be amplified or modified. To the Legislature, through its Public Accounts Committee, it will reveal in general how far the Government has complied with its expressed view in matters of importance and in particular how far moneys placed at the disposal of Government were regularly and properly spent. In order adequately to fulfil the latter function the report should, in addition to the points arising out of audit against provision of funds bring to notice of the Legislature, (1) important financial irregularities, such as deficiencies of sanction, failure to enforce or respect prescribed rules and procedure, offences against universally accepted standard of official conduct or financial administration, or any other class of irregularity, and (2) cases of losses, writes-off or nugatory expenditure."

22.8.4 The draft of all matter, in which it is proposed to question the action of the Finance Ministry or Department, is shown to the Finance Ministry or Department of the Government concerned before final inclusion in the Audit Report so that that department may have an opportunity of suggesting factual correction or modification. This is done as a matter of abundant precaution and is not obligatory. Great care is taken to ensure accuracy of facts of any case included in any Audit Report. Each fact is supported by a key document. The views of the Department concerned are also incorporated in the Report to make it as dispassionate a presentation as possible.

22.8.5 The Audit Report (Civil) relating to the Union Government contains the observations of the Comptroller and Auditor General on the Finance Accounts and Appropriation Accounts of the Union Government, apart from the individual cases of irregularities, etc. which the Comptroller and Auditor General deems important enough for inclusion in the Audit Report. The Finance Accounts are an Auditor's presentation of the general accounts of the Government to the Legislature giving some elucidation and some narrative presentation of new or salient features. Comments on the Finance Accounts relate to growth of revenues, growth of expenditure, magnitude of both internal and external debt, apart from a review of balances under debt. Deposit and Remittance heads. Observations of Audit on the Appropriation Account relate to unnecessary provisions, cases of excess, important cases of savings etc. with a view to convey a just and impartial picture of the financial position of the Government. There should be nothing in these observations by way of financial appreciation. Audit Report (Civil) of the Union Government also contains observations on the transactions of the grantees (autonomous bodies etc. which receive grants-in-aid from Government) so far as they relate to the grant received from Government.

22.8.6 Audit Report (Revenue Receipts) contains observations of the Comptroller and Auditor General about the collections of revenue, with reference to the statutory provisions and also their accounting. Important individual cases of irregularities in collection and accounting of revenue receipts are also included in the Audit Report (Revenue Receipts).

22.8.7 Audit Report (Railways) contains observations on the Appropriation Accounts of the Railways, apart from the individual cases of irregularities, etc. The Audit Report (Railways) also contains observations of the Comptroller and Auditor General on the Railway Finances as a whole.

22.8.8 Audit Report (Posts and Telegraphs) contains observations of the Comptroller and Auditor General on the

Appropriation Accounts of the Posts and Telegraphs Department and individual cases of irregularities in its financial transactions.

22.8.9 Audit Report (Defence Services) contains comments on the Appropriation Accounts of the Defence Services, in addition to individual cases of irregularities and comments on the working of the Ordnance Factories.

22.8.10 Audit Report (Civil), Audit Report (Revenue Receipts), Audit Report (Railways), Audit Report (Posts and Telegraphs) and Audit Report (Defence Services) are considered by the Public Accounts Committee.

22.8.11 Audit Report (Commercial) contains comments of the Comptroller and Auditor General on the working of the Public Sector undertakings comprising of Government Companies, Statutory Corporations, engaged in commercial activity, except those which are not under audit of the Comptroller and Auditor General according to the Acts creating them. An Audit Report (Commercial) contains comments of the Comptroller and Auditor General on the balance sheets as well as individual cases of irregularities. Audit Reports (Commercial) are considered by a separate Financial Committee of Parliament called Committee on Public Undertakings.

22.8.12 It may be mentioned in this connection, that apart from certain statutory corporations like Life Insurance Corporation which are not subject to audit by the Comptroller and Auditor General, there are some statutory corporations which are subject solely to audit by the Comptroller and Auditor General, i.e., Air India, Indian Airlines Corporation, Oil and Natural Gas Commission, etc., according to the relevant Acts setting them up. There are some other statutory corporations like State Financial Corporations, which are audited by professional auditors, but the Comptroller and Auditor General conducts superimposed audit over and above their audit.

22.8.13 The auditors of Government companies are appointed by Government on the advice of the Comptroller and Auditor General, according to the provisions of the Companies Act. That Act also empowers the Comptroller and Auditor General to issue directives to the professional auditors in regard to the manner in which the accounts of Government companies are to be audited by them. This ensures that the professional auditors perform their duties adequately, and on the basis of the results of their audit it is possible to appreciate properly the financial working of the Government companies. The Companies Act also gives the Comptroller and Auditor General the authority to conduct a supplementary audit of the accounts of Government companies, which is conducted more in the nature of Efficiency-cum-Performance Audit as against regularity audit.

22.8.14 In view of the huge investments in the public sector undertakings in the core sector of the economy, the importance of their accountability to Parliament/Legislature needs no emphasis. The audit by the professional auditors is not enough to secure this accountability as the same is designed in ensuring the correctness of the accounts only. The supplementary audit by the Comptroller and Auditor General being in the nature of efficiency-cum-performance audit plays an important role in enabling the Parliament/Legislature to review the performance and efficiency of the public sector undertakings.

Instead of going into the field covered by the professional auditors, the audit by the Comptroller and Auditor General is designed to find out whether a public sector undertaking has been able to fulfil the objective for which it has been established, whether targets set have been achieved, whether there has been any avoidable delay resulting in cost escalation, whether the value for money spent has been achieved, whether there has been any wasteful or extravagant expenditure, whether the dues have been realised efficiently and accurately in time, etc. For proper appraisal of the performance and efficiency of the public sector undertakings there is an Audit Board under the Chairmanship of a Deputy Comptroller and Auditor General. The Audit Board has got two full-time members, who are senior officers of the Indian Audit and Accounts Department. In addition, two part-time members are co-opted, from time to time, on the basis of technical and professional expertise needed for reviewing the performance of a particular public sector undertaking. These part-time members are appointed by the Administrative Ministry concerned with the concurrence of the Comptroller and Auditor General. Comprehensive appraisal report on the performance and efficiency of a public sector undertaking selected for review is prepared by the Commercial Audit Wing of the Indian Audit and Accounts Department on the basis of the appraisal made by the Audit Board. Such appraisals are included in the Audit Report (Commercial), which are laid in the Parliament.

22.9 The principles, procedures and methods of audit of Government transactions and preparation of Audit Reports mentioned earlier are applied *mutatis mutandis* by the Indian Audit and Accounts Department in auditing the transactions of Government companies and corporations, and other bodies or organisations which are audited by the Comptroller and Auditor General under the provisions of the Comptroller and Auditor General (Duties, Powers and Conditions of Service) Act, 1971. In addition, the provisions of the Companies Act, 1956 (in the cases of Government companies only), the provisions in the respective Legislations creating Government corporations, and the rules and regulations of such companies or corporations and those of other bodies or organizations are also taken into account by the Indian Audit and Accounts Department in auditing their accounts. The principles and methods of audit of commercial accounts are also taken into account by that Department, wherever necessary.

22.10 In the case of departmental commercial undertakings, the proforma accounts (Balance Sheet, Profit and Loss Account or Income and Expenditure Account) prepared by the departments concerned are also audited by the Indian Audit and Accounts Department applying the principles and methods of audit of commercial accounts, in addition to the audit of their transactions according to the principles, procedures and methods of audit of Government transactions.

22.11 It is needless to mention that the results of such elaborate audit are not only useful for ensuring accountability of the executive to Parliament/State Legislature, but are also helpful to the executive Government in enforcing compliance of its rules, regulations, orders etc. by its subordinate officials.

(v) PARLIAMENTARY/LEGISLATIVE SCRUTINY OF PUBLIC FINANCE THROUGH THE PUBLIC ACCOUNTS COMMITTEE AND THE COMMITTEE ON PUBLIC UNDERTAKINGS OF PARLIAMENT/LEGISLATURE

23.1 As mentioned in paragraph 21, the Estimates Committee is one of the three financial committees of the Parliament/Legislature which scrutinises the estimates prepared by different Ministries and Departments, in exercising control over public finance. The Parliamentary/Legislative scrutiny over public finance is exercised also through two other financial committees of the Parliament, namely the Public Accounts Committee and the Committee on Public Undertakings. The constitution and functioning of these two financial committees are discussed below.

23.2 Public Accounts Committee

23.2.1 It is the oldest and the most important Financial Committee of the Parliament. Public Accounts Committee was first set-up in India in 1921 with fifteen members. Initially, the Finance Member of the Governor General's Executive Council/Minister used to be the Chairman of the Public Accounts Committee. With the Constitution coming into force, since 1950 the Speaker of the Lok Sabha has been appointing one of the members of the Committee as its Chairman. Since 1954-55 the number of members of the Committee has been raised from 15 to 22, with the induction of seven members from the Rajya Sabha. Up to 1966 one of the members of the ruling party in the Committee used to be appointed as its Chairman. In 1967, a member of the opposition group was appointed as the Chairman of the Committee for the first time. Since then it has been a convention to appoint a member of the opposition group as the Chairman of the Public Accounts Committee. The term of the Committee is one year from May to April. The Chairman of the Committee is also appointed by the Speaker for one year.

23.2.2 *Functions of the Public Accounts Committee*

As mentioned in the book *Practice and Procedure of Parliament* (Kaul and Sakhder, 4th Edition), "The main function of the Committee is to examine the Appropriation Accounts showing the appropriation of sums granted by Parliament for the expenditure of the Government of India, the annual Finance Accounts of the Government of India and such other Accounts laid before the House as the Committee may think fit. In scrutinizing the Appropriation Accounts of the Government of India and the report of the Comptroller and Auditor General thereon, the Committee has to satisfy itself; that the moneys shown in the accounts as having been disbursed were legally available for, and applicable to, the service or purpose to which they have been applied or charged; that the expenditure conforms to the authority which governs it; and that every reappropriation has been made in accordance with the provisions made in this behalf under rules framed by competent authority.

The Committee has also to examine the statement of accounts showing the income and expenditure of State corporations, trading and manufacturing schemes, concerns and projects together with the balance-sheets and statements of profit and loss accounts which the President may have required to be prepared or are prepared under the provisions of the statutory rules regulating the financing of a particular corporation, trading or manufacturing scheme or concern or project and the report of the Comptroller and Auditor General thereon (excluding such public undertakings as has been allotted to the Committee on Public Undertakings); examine the statement of accounts showing the income and expenditure of autonomous and semi-autonomous bodies, the audit of which may be conducted by the Comptroller and Auditor General of India either under the directions of the President or by a statute of Parliament; and consider the report of the Comptroller and Auditor General in cases where the President may have required him to conduct an audit of any receipts or to examine the accounts of stores and stocks.

23.2.3 In addition to the above, the Public Accounts Committee examines each case in which money has been spent on any service during a financial year in excess of the amount granted by Parliament for that service for that year with reference to the facts and circumstances leading to such excess. The Committee makes suitable recommendations in a report for regularisation of all such excesses occurring in any financial year. In recommending regularisation of such excesses, quite often the Committee makes critical observations about the Ministries and Departments in which the excesses have occurred for their failure to prevent the excesses, but as a matter of convention recommends regularisation of all such excesses, subject to the critical observations made by it. Once the Public Accounts Committee makes recommendations for regularisation of the excesses. Demands for excess grants are presented to the House to cover the excess expenditure.

23.2.4 As mentioned in the book *Practice and Procedure of Parliament* (Kaul and Sakhder, 4th Edition), "The functions of the Committee extend beyond the formality of expenditure to 'its wisdom, faithfulness and economy'. The Committee thus examines cases involving losses, nugatory expenditure and financial irregularities. When any case of proved negligence resulting in loss or extravagance is brought to the notice of the Committee, the ministry concerned is called upon to explain as to what action, disciplinary or otherwise, has been taken to prevent a recurrence. In such cases the Committee also records its opinion either disapproving the action of Government or passing strictures against the extravagance or lack of proper control by the Ministry or Department concerned.

Another important function of the Committee is the discussion of points of financial discipline and principle."

It has also been mentioned in the book *Practice and Procedure of Parliament* (Kaul and Sakhder, 4th Edition), "that the Public Accounts Committee has of its own accord inquired into various irregularities which have become public or which have been brought to the notice of the Government, even though no formal Audit Report was presented on the subjects." It would thus appear that although usually the Public Accounts Committee functions with reference to the Accounts and Audit Reports presented to Parliament by the Comptroller and Auditor General, the Committee may and does take up *suo motto* for examination even cases which have not been mentioned in any Audit Report. In this context, an important question arises whether any case involving public finance which has become public and subject matter of discussions in Parliament, it should stand automatically referred to the Parliament's Financial Committee concerned, viz., Public Accounts Committee or the Committee on Public Undertakings (only if the case relates to a public undertaking). On the other hand, it may also be for consideration of the Comptroller and Auditor General whether any Audit Report may or needs to be presented in respect of a case about which Parliament is already seized, keeping in view the following aspects:

(i) His Reports are laid before Parliament for its consideration. When the Parliament is already seized of a matter, an Audit Report on it may not receive the importance and attention which is normally given to an Audit Report. Besides, if Parliament, in its wisdom, decides to set up a Joint Parliamentary Committee or any other authority to probe into the matter, consideration of an Audit Report on that matter may become a mere formality, if not redundant.

(ii) When Parliament is seized of a matter relating to public finance, usually lot of dust is raised due to allegations and counter-allegations. The atmosphere thus becomes charged with emotion, and may not, therefore, be conducive for dispassionate and objective examination of an Audit Report in the matter. Keeping in view the need for safeguarding the objectivity, impartiality and impersonal attitude of the Audit Department, it may not be in the interest of that Department to get itself involved in the volatile situation by presenting an Audit Report, which is unlikely to serve the purpose for which it is meant.

23.2.5 The Public Accounts Committee is more concerned with the failure in system or the control mechanism which facilitated the loss, defalcation or wastage rather than the individuals involved. But the Committee satisfies itself that the Ministry/Department has taken necessary action, after conducting such enquiry as the occasion demanded, including appropriate disciplinary action against delinquent official or officials. The Committee usually deals with such cases with an impersonal attitude. There is an established convention in the Audit Department of not mentioning the names of individuals or private parties in the Audit Reports. Similarly, the Public Accounts Committee also does not concern itself with any individual or private party, but satisfies itself about the adequacy of the action taken against individuals or private parties involved in any loss, wastage, defalcation, etc. If the Committee so feels, it comments on the adequacy of the action taken in the matter.

23.2.6 Besides, the Public Accounts Committee does not concern itself with any policy of Government. But the Committee points out such cases where there has been extravagance, waste or loss in implementing a policy, even if the policy itself was beyond reproach or when the policy itself proved to be faulty and led to waste or loss etc.

23.2.7 *Working of the Public Accounts Committee*

Immediately, after the Public Accounts Committee is constituted for a year, a preliminary sitting is held to consider the programme of work for the year. The programme for sittings of the Committee is drawn up by its Secretariat. The programme so drawn up needs the approval of the Chairman of the Committee.

An informal meeting is also arranged for discussions with the Comptroller and Auditor General or his deputy dealing with the Audit Reports about the more important points arising out of the Accounts and the Audit Reports. With the passage of time the number of cases for consideration has increased and it is not possible for the Public Accounts Committee to examine all the cases arising out of the Accounts and the Audit Reports with the same intensity. It, therefore, categorises, in consultation with the Comptroller and Auditor General or senior officers of his department the cases in three categories, viz., most important, important and not so important so that the working groups may accordingly select cases for in-depth study devoting greater attention to the more important cases.

Till about mid-nineteen seventies, the Public Accounts Committee used to select the more important cases in the Audit Reports for taking evidence. In the remaining cases it used to make its recommendations after obtaining from Government written replies, information and documents. In this process, there used to be recommendation of the Public Accounts Committee on each of the cases mentioned in the Audit Reports. Presently, due to paucity of time, the Public Accounts Committee usually makes its recommendations on a selective basis.

The Public Accounts Committee is assisted by the Comptroller and Auditor General from time to time in the following manner:

(i) 'Memoranda of important points' are furnished by the office of the Comptroller and Auditor General to the Public Accounts Committee on all the important points arising out of the accounts and the cases reported in the Audit Reports indicating the possible questions which may be asked from the Ministries and Departments.

(ii) The information, details and documents furnished by the Ministries and Departments are factually verified by the office of the Comptroller and Auditor General so that there is no dispute about them at a later stage.

(iii) The Members of the Committee or the study group entrusted with any particular subject are briefed by the senior officers of the Indian Audit and Accounts Department about the important points and the line of examination of the cases selected for consideration of the Public Accounts Committee.

(iv) In each day of sitting of the Committee, the Chairman is briefed in his chamber by the senior officers of the Indian Audit and Accounts Department for some time, before the sitting commences, about the case or cases to be taken up by the Committee on that day.

(v) The Comptroller and Auditor General is usually present in the sittings of the Public Accounts Committee in which evidence is taken from Departmental witnesses. His wisdom and valuable counsel are always available to the Committee. That is why he is said to be the friend, philosopher and guide of the Public Accounts Committee. He intervenes, with the consent of the Chairman, if there is any attempt on the part of Departmental witnesses to circumvent the real issues. Quite often the Chairman requests the Comptroller and Auditor General to give his opinion or advice on certain points under deliberation. He also assists the Committee by intervening in time if the deliberations of the Committee tend to go off the track from real issues by briefing the Chairman, on whose right side he sits.

(vi) The officials concerned of the Indian Audit and Accounts Department who are acquainted with facts and documents relating to the case or cases under deliberation of the Public Accounts Committee remain present throughout the sitting of the Committee along with the documents relevant to these cases so that these may be produced instantly, whenever required by the Chairman during the sitting.

In an article 'Public Accounts Committee—An Admirable Institution' published in the Golden Jubilee (1921-71) Souvenir of the Public Accounts Committee, Late A.K. Chanda, former

Comptroller and Auditor General aptly described the relation between the Audit Department and the Public Accounts Committee in the following words:

> "...The effectiveness of Audit depended on the endorsement it received from the Committee; likewise, the effectiveness of the Committee depended on the thoroughness and circumspection with which audit had been conducted and its report compiled. Thus the Committee and I functioned in a refreshing atmosphere of mutual respect, understanding, accord and harmony."
> This relation has been continuing.

Whenever considered necessary, the Public Accounts Committee appoints a Sub-Committee to examine any matter of importance arising out of the Accounts and the Audit Reports presented to Parliament by the Comptroller and Auditor General. According to the book *Practice and Procedure of Parliament* (Kaul and Sakhder, 4th Edition) a Sub-Committee, so appointed, "has the powers of the Committee as a whole and any report of the sub-Committee, after the Committee's approval, is deemed to be the report of the whole Committee." Apart from this, the Public Accounts Committee constitutes an 'Action Taken Sub-Committee', consisting of the convenors of the different working groups of the Committee, to examine the replies of Government to the recommendations of the Committee contained in its earlier Reports and prepare a further report on such replies containing suitable recommendations.

The Chairman of the Public Accounts Committee also appoints different working groups, in consultation with the members of the Committee for intensive examination of different subjects selected by the Committee for its examination. The Chairman chooses the members of each working group taking into account the known aptitudes of the members and other relevant factors. The Chairman also appoints one of the members of each working group to act as its convenor, who acts as its leader and presides over its sittings. The working groups work in an informal manner and do not prepare any report. However, each working group examines the draft report prepared by the Secretariat on the subject allotted to it, before the same is submitted to the Committee for approval.

The Public Accounts Committee also undertakes on-the-spot study tours, with the approval of the Speaker for an assessment of the actual working of an office, organisation, institution etc. Such study tours may also be undertaken by the Sub-Committees or the working groups.

In connection with the cases selected by it, the Public Accounts Committee calls departmental officials to give evidence in connection with its examination of the cases of a particular Ministry/Department relating to the Accounts and the Audit Reports. Usually, the Secretary of the Ministry concerned appears before the Public Accounts Committee. In case it is not possible for him to appear before the Committee for some unavoidable reason, he informs the Chairman about it and deputes a senior officer, not below the rank of Joint Secretary, to give evidence.

23.2.8 The verbatim proceedings of all the sittings of the Public Accounts Committee are recorded. After examination of the Accounts and the Audit Reports are completed, and the additional information required by the Committee has been received, the Secretariat of the Committee prepares the draft report taking into account the verbatim proceedings of the sittings of the Committee, evidence of the departmental witnesses and the written information and documents obtained from the Ministries and Departments. A copy of the draft report is sent to the Comptroller and Auditor General for factual verification. A copy of this draft report is also submitted to the Chairman for approval. The draft report, as approved by the Chairman, is considered in a sitting of the Committee. The Comptroller and Auditor General is also present at this sitting to point out the amendments that may be necessary in the facts and figures. A convention has developed in India for submission of unanimous reports by the Public Accounts Committee. It is said that the Public Accounts Committee functions as a mini-Parliament in its working. In the Public Accounts Committee, however, all the members rise above the partyline and act in unison for better financial health of the nation. The reports of the Committee are submitted to the Lok Sabha by the Chairman himself or by a member authorised to do so by the Chairman. In the Rajya Sabha, a member of the Committee from that House submits the reports. The reports of the Public Accounts Committee are usually adopted by both Houses of the Parliament without any discussion, although it is open to the Lok Sabha to discuss reports of the Committee.

23.2.9 It is mentioned in the book *Practice and Procedure of Parliament* (Kaul and Sakhder, 4th Edition) that the recommendations of the Public Accounts Committee "are treated with respect by the Government and most of them are accepted and implemented. In the event of any disagreement between the Government and the Committee in regard to any recommendation contained in the report of the Committee, the Government have, in the first instance, to apprise the Committee of the reasons that might have weighed with them in not accepting or implementing a recommendation." It states further that, "The Action Taken Sub-Committee of the Public Accounts Committee examines the 'Action Taken' notes received from the Ministries/Departments and draws up separate 'Action Taken' reports which are subsequently adopted by the main Committee and presented to the House. Before finalising its report, the Action Taken Sub-Committee can call the representatives of the Ministries/Departments for informal discussions and thus obtain clarification on points arising out of the notes furnished by the Government and also speed up the replies where they have not been received." The 'Action Taken' reports are submitted to the Lok Sabha and Rajya Sabha like the original reports to which they relate.

23.2.10 The importance of the Public Accounts Committee of the Parliament has been expressed in the following words in November 1971 by the then President of India in his message on the occasion of the Golden Jubilee celebrations of the Committee:

> "The Public Accounts Committee in India came into lively arena of our parliamentary life only after independent India's Constitution came into force. With universal adult franchise, our Parliament and State Legislatures became the real custodians of executive power and conduct. The Public Accounts Committee has the power to summon and question civil servants in order to ensure that the money voted is properly spent. The fear of exposure in the process of such questioning serves in itself as a sure deterrent against wrong actions. In its work, the Committee has the advice and unrivalled assistance of one of the most important functionaries under our Constitution, the Comptroller and Auditor General. Viewed in this background, I have doubt that the Public Accounts

Committee of our Parliament has a record of which it can be legitimately proud."

23.2.11 This place of pride has been achieved by the Committee gradually due to its impartial and objective attitude in dealing with the cases arising out of the Accounts and the Audit Reports. This will be evident from the recollections of Late T.N. Singh who was a member and Chairman of the Public Accounts Committee for about a decade, as recorded in his article 'My Experience of the Public Accounts Committee' appearing in the Golden Jubilee (1921-71) Souvenir of the Public Accounts Committee. He recalled as follows:

> "...because it was considered to be principally a post-mortem both examining accounts of expenditure incurred many years ago, the Public Accounts Committee was considered by Members to be a body of very little importance. Standing Committees of the various Ministries were then considered to be important Committees and there used to be a scramble for their membership. Being a new member to Parliament, it was natural for me to be left out of these Standing Committees. I was elected to the Public Accounts Committee because so few wanted to be there."

When the Budget session of 1950 was about to come to a close, Sri Satya Narain Sinha, the then Minister of Parliamentary Affairs rather apologetically offered me membership of the Public Accounts Committee. When I agreed to his suggestion, many of my colleagues expressed that "I, a senior Congressman, had agreed to be the member of a Committee which only carried out examination of three or four-year old accounts." This was the position in 1950, immediately after the Constitution came into effect.

But Late T.N. Singh continued to recall, "However, it did not take me long to realise how very important role this Committee would play in nurturing and strengthening India's young democracy....

After a few months' work in the Public Accounts Committee, I came to realise that for upholding democracy and parliamentary control over expenditure, it had to play an increasingly important role..."

He went to conclude, "The Public Accounts Committee by its close scrutiny of accounts has earned a reputation for impartiality, firmness, and a grasp for details. The good work done by this Committee has helped greatly in improving financial control by the Administration and assisted in the detection of many irregularities and even 'dishonesties'."

23.3 Committee on Public Undertakings

23.3.1 With the introduction of the planned economic development of the country, there were large investments by Government in setting up public undertakings in the core sector. In view of the large investments made from the Consolidated Fund, a feeling grew in the Parliament that the performance of such public undertakings should be subjected to Parliamentary/Legislative scrutiny. As mentioned in the book *Practice and Procedure of Parliament* (Kaul and Sakhder, 4th Edition), in December 1953, the then Speaker of the Lok Sabha G.V. Mavalankar wrote to the Prime Minister conveying that there was a general feeling in favour of appointing a standing parliamentary committee to examine the working of autonomous public corporations. The matter remained under consideration for several years, and in November 1961 Government decided to appoint a Joint Committee on public undertaking. However, the Committee on Public Undertakings was constituted for the first time with effect from 1st May 1964.

23.3.2 Initially, the Committee on Public Undertakings had 15 members—10 from the Lok Sabha and 5 from the Rajya Sabha. In 1974-75, the strength of the Committee was raised to 22, 15 from Lok Sabha and 7 from the Rajya Sabha. The Chairman of the Committee on Public Undertakings is appointed by the Speaker from amongst the members of the Committee. The term of office of the members of the Committee is one year. The Chairman is also appointed for one year.

23.3.3 According to the book *Practice and Procedure of Parliament* (Kaul and Sakhder, 4th Edition), the functions of the Committee are:

"(a) to examine the reports and accounts of such public undertakings as have been specifically allotted to the Committee for this purpose;

(b) to examine the reports, if any, of the Comptroller and Auditor General on public undertakings;

(c) to examine, in the context of the autonomy and efficiency of public undertakings, whether the affairs of the public undertakings are being managed in accordance with sound business principles and prudent commercial policies; and

(d) to exercise such other functions vested in the Public Accounts Committee and the Estimates Committee in relation to the public undertakings specified for the Committee as are not covered by clauses (a), (b) and (c) above and as may be allotted to the Committee by the Speaker from time to time.

The Committee does not examine and investigate any of the following:

(i) matters of major Government policy as distinct from business or commercial functions of the public undertakings; or

(ii) matters of day to day administrations; and matter for the consideration of which machinery is established by any special statute under which a particular public undertakings is established.

The examination of public undertakings by the Committee is "generally in the nature of an evaluation of the performance of an undertaking covering all aspects like implementation of policies, programmes, management, financial working etc."

23.3.4 *Working of the Committee on Public Undertakings*

The Committee selects, at the beginning of each term, the subjects to be examined by it. The Committee has a practice also to select a few subjects in advance for examination in the next term. While some of the undertakings are selected for full-fledged in-depth study, some others are selected for limited study. In the cases selected for limited study, the Chairman is authorised to obtain information required from the undertaking concerned without any reference to the Committee.

The Committee on Public Undertakings asks the administrative Ministry or the undertaking concerned, which has been selected for study, to furnish preliminary material for use by the members of the Committee. Such material received from the Ministry or undertaking is circulated to the members. The members study the material and frame questions or points on which they require further information. The Secretariat of the Committee independently examines the material and also frames questions or points on which further information is to be collected. Based on its own scrutiny and also questions or points indicated by the members, the secretariat prepares a questionnaire for examination of the undertaking. The questionnaire so prepared is circulated to the members, after the same has been approved by the Chairman. The same questionnaire is also sent to the administrative Ministry and the undertaking will before the sitting scheduled for taking evidence of the representatives of the administrative Ministry and the undertaking. If the Committee is not able to take complete evidence in its scheduled sitting, the remaining information is obtained in writing. The information so received is circulated to the members.

The Committee on Public Undertakings also obtains memoranda from non-official organisations, such as Chambers of Commerce, trade organisations, professional consultants, private sector companies in the same field as also the registered trade unions of workers and employees of the undertaking. When the Committee visits the undertaking, the Committee gives an opportunity to the representatives of the registered trade unions of workers and employees to express their views. While the unions are not allowed to represent on any individual case or any matter relating to individual dispute, their views on matters like efficiency, economy, productivity, cost of production, avoidance of waste are duly considered.

In addition to examination of individual undertakings selected by it, the Committee also examines matters or problems which are common to all the undertakings. For such a horizontal study, information is obtained from all the undertakings for the particular matter or problem.

The Committee on Public Undertakings forms study groups for in-depth study of selected subjects. The Committee also undertakes study tours. During the study tours, the Committee holds discussions amongst itself or with field officers, but no decisions are taken in such sittings.

23.3.5 The Committee also selects for examination matters raised in the Audit Reports of the Comptroller and Auditor General on the public undertakings which have been taken up for its study. For such matters raised in the Audit Reports, the Committee is assisted by the Comptroller and Auditor General or his representatives. On such matters, Audit Department sends to the Committee 'Memorandum of Important Points', indicating the possible lines of enquiry and the questions which may be raised. The Committee frames the questions on such matters on the basis of the details available in the Audit Report and the Memorandum of Important Points. Before the Committee takes evidence of departmental officials on such matters the Comptroller and Auditor General or his representatives brief the Committee on these matters. When the Committee takes evidence of the officials of the undertaking concerned or of the administrative Ministry on such matters arising out of the Audit Report, the Comptroller and Auditor-General or his representatives remain present to assist the Committee in its deliberations. The Comptroller and Auditor General also intervenes, with the permission of the Chairman, whenever he feels that such intervention is necessary. He may also ask questions, with the permission of the Chairman, to get clarification on some points from the official witness. However, the Comptroller and Auditor General or his representatives remain present in a sitting only when evidence is taken on matter arising out of the Audit Report. As soon as that is over, he and his representatives present in the meeting withdraw from the Committee room.

23.3.6 The Committee on Public Undertakings takes evidence of the officials in two stages. In the first stage, evidence of the representatives of the undertaking is taken by the Committee on matters relating to management or working of the undertaking. In the second stage, evidence of the officials of the administrative Ministry is taken on policy matters or such other matters for which the administrative Ministry is responsible. The representatives of the administrative Ministry are not allowed to be present when the Committee takes evidence of the officials of the undertaking. Similarly, when the evidence of the representatives of the administrative Ministry is taken, the officials of the undertaking are not allowed to be present.

23.3.7 On the basis of the conclusions reached by the Committee on a subject, a draft report is prepared by the Secretariat of the Committee. After the Chairman's approval copies of the draft report are sent to the members of the Committee. Thereafter, the draft report is considered in a sitting of the Committee. A copy of the draft report, so far as it relates to matters arising out of the Audit Report, is sent to the Comptroller and Auditor General for factual verification. A copy of the draft report, without the draft recommendations, is also sent to the administrative Ministry for factual verification. At this stage, the draft report is treated as secret. The Chairman makes necessary amendments in the draft report on the basis of the comments of the Comptroller and Auditor General and the administrative Ministry. If these factual amendments necessitate amendments in the recommendations in the draft report already approved by the Committee, the Chairman places the matter before the Committee. An authenticated copy of its report of the Committee is presented to the Lok Sabha by the Chairman or his representative. Similarly, an authenticated copy of the report is submitted to the Rajya Sabha by a member of the Committee from that House.

23.3.8 After presentation of the report in both the Houses of Parliament, copies of the report are sent to the administrative Ministry and the undertaking for furnishing replies to the recommendations of the Committee. The replies received from them are examined by the 'Action Taken Sub-Committee' of the Committee on Public Undertakings. The Action Taken Sub-Committee is headed by the Chairman of the Committee. This Sub-Committee examines the replies furnished by the undertaking and the administrative Ministry and prepares an Action Taken Report with further recommendations, whenever necessary, on the basis of replies received on original recommendations. The Action Taken Report is also submitted to both Houses of the Parliament.

5

Epilogue

24. From the narration given in the earlier chapters, it would appear that a very elaborate system exists for Parliamentary/ Legislative control, Executive control and Audit control over public finances in India. The question that may arise in this connection is how effective the system has been in regulating the public finance. In considering this aspect we have to bear in mind that, however, perfect a system is, it becomes bad when it is worked by people who are bad. Again the people who work the system come from the society for which the system functions. If the number of bad people who work the system is more than those who are good, it only indicates that the society itself has more bad people than the good ones. After all, the composition of Government which operates the system is only reflection of the society which it serves. This is certainly not a place to discus how to change the composition of the society with good people than bad ones.

24.1 Perhaps there was no stage of human society when it was completely devoid of bad people; possibly, only the number has varied from time to time. As such, despite the best of systems, frauds and losses due to human aberration cannot be altogether eliminated. For example, a cashier may run away with money while bringing the same from the Treasury or Bank, or he may be waylaid by a robber who takes away the money. Apart from aberrations, there may be human failures also. The cashier is forgetful and leaves the cash unlocked while going for a short-while to attend a telephone call and finds on return that the cash is gone. That is human failure. There may also be a case in which fraud or loss due to human aberration in one, is facilitated by the human failure on the part of another. Let us take a mundane example. Under the system, a bill drawn by a Drawing and

Disbursing Officer is required to be entered in a Bill Register, before it is sent to the Treasury or Bank for encashment, so that the Drawing and Disbursing Officer is able to keep watch over its encashment and entry in the cash book after encashment. The Drawing and Disbursing Officer fails to ensure that a particular bill is entered in the Bill Register when he passes the same. The cashier encashes the bill and pockets the money. The fraud may remain undetected for a long time, as it is not possible for the Drawing and Disbursing Officer to remember all the bills he has passed. In this case, the aberration in the cashier for pocketing the money is facilitated by the failure on the part of the Drawing and Disbursing Officer. Broadly speaking, however, such human aberration is also human failure.

24.2 It may not be possible to fully eliminate human failure, but with proper development of human resources it is certainly possible to minimise it. We, however, failed to do so when the need arose. For example, we had an excellent poverty alleviation scheme in the Integrated Rural Development Programme (IRDP). The scheme was to be implemented jointly by State Governments and the Banks. The desired results of IRDP could not be achieved because we did not have the right personnel to implement the programme both in State Governments and in Banks. Besides, we also failed to educate the intended beneficiaries to reap the benefit of the programme. At the risk of repetition, I would like to reproduce below my views in this respect, which were incorporated by Shri G.N.S. Raghavan in his book *Development and Communication in India* (First Edition, 1992),

"IRDP is designed in such a manner that its success lies in sincere and effective participation of three agencies, viz., banks. Government agencies including panchayats, and the beneficiary for. IRDP has failed to a large extent due to failures of all the three participants, as indicated below:

1. Banks

(i) The concept that banking is now an instrument of national developmental efforts has not reached the lower echelon of banks, including rural banks. The result is that the IRDP beneficiaries are treated by them like other borrowers and not as beneficiaries of a development activity of which the banks themselves are participants. Instead of being of assistance to the IRDP beneficiaries, banks become instruments of harassment to the beneficiaries, where they have to make several rounds to get their dues in the shape of subsidy, inputs or loans.

(ii) Taking advantage of the simplicity and ignorance of rules and procedures of the beneficiaries, a class of touts has grown in the rural sector which acts as the go-between, with encouragement from the unscrupulous among bankers. Beneficiaries are often thus exploited by both the touts and the banks.

(iii) The flow of inputs in the shape of loan, subsidy or material rarely in time. This seriously affects income generation.

(iv) When the assistance is in the form of materials, banks and government agencies connive in such a manner that the beneficiaries more often do not get it of full value. The balance goes to add to the volume of black money.

(v) Banks insist on security before disbursement of loans, although the IRDP provides for security in the shape of assets created out of assistance only.

(vi) Banks often try to recover dues without any reference to income generation.

2. *Government Agencies*

(i) No survey is conducted which should be the basis of identification and selection of beneficiaries; as a result, identification is more on *ad hoc* rather than any scientific basis.

(ii) Because of (i) above, the selection of schemes for an individual beneficiary is faulty, without any reference to his ability and aptitude.

(iii) There is no monitoring either from the side of government agencies or the banks to find out whether the beneficiaries are able to generate enough income to take them beyond the poverty line.

(iv) There is no ongoing guidance or assistance to the beneficiaries to enable them to execute the schemes in a manner to generate stipulated income. Consequently, income generation does not take place and the capital base is steadily eroded, leaving the beneficiary in a debt trap.

(v) Flow of funds to the implementing agencies is not need-based. More often the flow of funds takes place towards the latter half of the financial year.

3. Beneficiaries

(i) Because of their ignorance, the beneficiaries have no say in the schemes selected for them. The schemes are often unsuited to their circumstances and ability.

(ii) They fall victims of greed for easy money and become perpetual debtors."

24.3 IRDP is an isolated instance. There will be instances galore of such failures if we make in-depth review of all aspects of our developmental projects and programmes, instead of mostly confining the reviews to financial transactions only, because apart from financial transactions by themselves, there are many other aspects which ultimately affect public finance.

25.1 Apart from human failure there may be failure of systems also. A system develops to cater to the needs of particular circumstances. If the circumstances change, the existing system may not suit the new circumstances. We inherited our administrative system from Britishers, who had designed it to safeguard their interest, particularly because they had to depend mostly on us to work the system. Thus the system that we inherited was excellent so far as safeguarding financial transactions which were concentrated in few places and meant for mainly administrative purposes. After independence the circumstances vastly changed with more emphasis on developmental expenditure. We failed to update the system to meet the needs of the changed circumstances. For example, consequent on nationalisation of banks, there was great expansion of the banking system with sudden increase of the number of public sector bank branches, many of them even in remote rural areas. This was needed to make the banks active participants in the developmental activities in the country. The system of regulation of banking which was prevalent before such expansion of banking activities was not changed to meet the new circumstances. As a result, the intensity of regulatory function and inspection of banks by the Reserve Bank of India perhaps may not have been possible to be maintained. On the other hand, internal inspection and regulatory function of the respective banks perhaps did not also develop to take care of the large number of new branches, many of which were in rural areas. As a result, it is alleged, there was serious system failures which are stated to be the main reasons for the multi-crore rupees scam in the banking industry in the recent past.

25.2 This is only one area. There are many such areas where we failed to update the system to cater for the changed circumstances and which adversely affected public finance.

26.1 Apart from human failure and system failure mentioned earlier, the other factor which affects executive control over public finance in a major way is corruption. Speaking in a general way, corruption, in the context of public finance, is acceptance of illegal gratification by misusing official position in granting an undue favour which affects public finance. Sometimes one is not even aware where the corruption starts and how exactly it affects public finance, the link being very obscure or tenuous. For example, before Diwali one may find cars belonging to companies or business houses loaded with packets of sweets or dry-fruits or other gifts are doing the rounds of the Government residential colonies for distributing them at select houses, which is apparently innocuous or too small a matter to be taken notice of. But then the question remains why these gifts have gone only to a few select houses and not all the houses in the colony! A critical look at the selection of houses for distribution of these small gifts will point out that the residents of these houses are in positions which may be of use to the distributors of the gifts, say for example, in an economic Ministry or an office subordinate to an economic Ministry. The purpose behind distribution of such gifts obviously is to gain or renew acquaintance or approach, which may be of use some time in future. One may argue is he or she purchasable with a packet of sweets or dry-fruits! But then, has he or she asked himself/herself whether the same gift packet would have come had he/she been in another position, say in the Ministry of Education, or Department of Social Welfare. (This practice of giving gifts and accepting the same has since attracted the notice of the Central Vigilance Commission; acceptance of such gifts, it is understood, is now banned). Let us also look at it from a different angle. A single gift packet may not be of any significant value. But the total cost of all such gift packets distributed at least twice a year by all such companies, business houses, contractors, traders, etc., is quite substantial. This amount would have contributed to their profit and thus inflated the amount of tax payable by them. In this way, these gift packets affect public finance, may be in a minuscule way. There are people who will laugh at this proposition. But then, as stated before, more often one does not even ponder over the origin of corruption. However, the very purpose of writing this is to just indicate how tolerant society has gradually become to corruption. A few other such small things (!) which have perhaps come to be tolerated are invitation to expensive dinners and cocktail parties in expensive hotels, arrangements for free transports, etc.

26.2 Corruption had spread its tentacles in the Indian society in a perceptible way during the Second World War days. It had affected the bureaucracy even at that time, but did not reach much higher level. In the recent years, however, allegations and counter-allegations about 'scams', 'kickbacks' etc., involving huge amounts, are being raised both inside the Parliament and outside, which implicate even the decision making process. The post-independence policy has taken such a turn that all the political parties are alleged to be dependent on contributions from business houses, companies, traders, contractors, etc., in a big way, whichever party is in power being the alleged recipient of the biggest share. As a result, it is alleged, the decision making process is affected in granting undue favour by whichever party is in power to the contributors of the funds. Such concessions affect public finance in the shape of excess payments for services or lesser collection of dues to Government. The moneys alleged to be contributed to the political parties are mostly unaccounted for; had they been accounted for, there would have been more receipts in public finance in the shape of taxes on profits. Besides, such huge amounts of unaccounted for money add to the inflationary conditions in the country. These allegations and counter-allegations about 'scams', 'kick-backs' have reached a serious proportion. It is high time all right thinking people in different political parties sit together and put an end to this practice. Only then will it be possible to make serious attempts to eradicate corruption from other spheres. In doing so, we will have to ask ourselves, each one of us, whether we are ourselves honest, before pointing accusing fingers towards others.

27. The other areas *inter alia* which invite attention for better management of public finance are:

(i) Accuracy is *sine qua non* for budgeting. Each year, the Comptroller and Auditor General points out a number of cases in which there have been savings and excesses under different Demands for Grants. The excesses require regularization by Parliament on the basis of the recommendations of the Public Accounts Committee (paragraph 23.2.3) and, as such, come under scrutiny. The cases of savings are usually not subjected to such scrutiny. But the cases of savings are no less reprehensible, as over estimation in a demand for Grant in which the saving has occurred is responsible for lesser or no provision for another important service or scheme.

(ii) There should be a stop to the window dressing of the budget and accounts to depict a picture, which is far from the reality.

For example, a tendency is discernible to provide for lesser expenditure on capital account to show lesser budgetary deficit, in an attempt to camouflage an increase in Revenue Deficit due to increase in revenue expenditure as compared to revenue receipts. In reality, however, the lesser budgetary deficit in such an event is not indicative of any improvement in the financial health of the country; rather the increase in revenue deficit is harmful for it.

Similarly, if the loan granted to a public sector unit is converted into share capital to show its financial position better, it does not in anyway improve its working. With the conversion of the loan into share capital, its liability to repay the loan and interest thereon is extinguished. As such, its accounts will show better financial results, which is not the real position. On the other hand, public finance is affected due to non-repayment of loan and interest which would have been otherwise payable by the public sector unit.

These are only illustrative and not exhaustive examples of how window dressing of budget and accounts is sometimes done.

(iii) As mentioned earlier, many of the Demands for Grants gets approved by the Lok Sabha without any discussion, due to lack of time for discussions of all the Demands for Grants. It is for consideration whether some way may be devised so that each of the Demands for Grants comes under discussions even if for a limited time, within the overall time limit, if necessary by subjecting them to detailed scrutiny by several small groups of Lok Sabha members outside the Parliament's working hours.

(iv) With the increase in developmental activities Government transactions have increased enormously over the years. As a result, the attention of the Indian Audit and Accounts Department has naturally been more on efficiency-cum-performance audit rather than on regularity audit. Besides, due to the developmental activities, the number of field offices of various departments and their spread have increased making it perhaps difficult for the Indian Audit and Accounts Department to arrange for their audit with the same intensity and periodicity which it followed earlier. It is true, regularity audit discloses irregularities involving small amounts, but this is also essential for maintaining the financial discipline. If a large number of such irregularities involving small amounts remain undetected, an attitude of 'nothing happens' is bound to grow in the bureaucracy leading to more and more of such irregularities. If over the years it has been found that it is not possible for the Indian Audit and Accounts Department to conduct regularity audit with the earlier intensity and periodicity, the alternative may be to strengthen internal audit in those departments where it exists or to introduce internal audit in other departments, where it does not exist.

(v) Ideally, the Executive should accept Audit as a friend and treat its criticisms in right spirit. In fact, if the executive attends promptly to the irregularities pointed by Audit and takes action against the delinquent officials in time that will go a long way in maintaining financial discipline, which should be the aim of both the Executive and Audit. Unfortunately, the Executive in India has not been able to view Audit as a friend. Audit is treated by the Executive as a stumbling block, if not an enemy. In most cases, audit objections, therefore, remain unattended. The bias against Audit is sometimes so intense that the Executive brazenly ventures in defending an indefensible case even at the stage when the matter is under consideration of the Public Accounts Committee. This will be evident from the following extract, from the observations of R.R. Morarka, Ex-chairman, Public Accounts Committee (1962-64) in his article, 'P.A.C.—How to Make It More Effective' published in the Golden Jubilee (1921-1971) Souvenir of the Public Accounts Committee.

"But, in any case, there is no room for indefensible defence, which is put up today by the Secretaries and Departmental Heads appearing before the P.A.C. It has been found that even in admittedly indefensible cases, officials as high as the Secretaries would come before the Committee and consider it their duty to defend these transactions. It is difficult to imagine that such highly-trained and experienced senior officers would not realise the mistakes of their subordinates. It is still more difficult to understand why seasoned and loyal officers should go to such lengths to defend the delinquent officers.

No doubt, the senior officers, as stated earlier, are responsible for the transactions in their Departments and they should also give protection to their juniors. But a line must be drawn between cases involving *bona fide* mistakes or errors of judgement and those irregularities involving corruption, *mala fide*, malpractice, negligence or repetition of the same type of irregularities. In fact, the stout defence which is often put up by the departmental heads, indirectly encourages the officers in committing irregularities, which the P.A.C is keen to root out.

At the risk of repetition, I would say that the executive officers must be given all protection which they deserve for their *bona fide* actions, but in the case of questionable transactions, the Secretary or the Departmental Head should consider himself equally responsible and duty bound to put the facts before the PAC and Parliament, as his loyalty to the cause should be certainly higher than that to his colleagues or to an individual."

The above observations of an ex-chairman of the Public Accounts Committee are equally applicable to the Executive in its dealing with Audit objections.

(vi) Lastly, there is urgent need for intensifying the process of imparting training to the members of bureaucracy at all levels in constitutional provisions, laws, rules, procedures, etc., relating to public finance to not only guard against human failures and system failures but also to imbibe in them the need for financial disciplines in national interest.

For example, most of the heads of departments these days are technocrats. With the enormous increase in financial transactions in their departments, it has become necessary for them, for proper financial administration, to be broadly acquainted with the constitutional provisions, laws, rules, procedures etc. relating to public finance, instead of being completely dependent on their finance and accounts officers.

Again much of the functions of the Treasury Officer are now performed by a Manager of a branch of a public sector bank entrusted with Government transactions. The Manager of the branch of such a Bank does not have the training and experience of a Treasury Officer. It is, therefore, necessary that such Bank Managers are given appropriate training for dealing with Government transactions.

These instances are only illustrative and not exhaustive.

28. Gone are days, when the transactions relating to public finance could be left to a few experts in the field. Public finance has become now a subject of much wider interest because of the widespread misuse of public finance for personal gains or political gains etc., with impunity. Not only that, those who are involved in such misdeeds continue to occupy important positions in administration and/or get elected to Parliament or State Legislature with money and muscle power. As a result, an attitude of 'nothing happens' has been gaining ground making the honest ones more and more diffident, while others are becoming more daring to commit such irregularities, taking advantage, in many cases, of the delayed justice system. Because of the latter ones being in power, the honest ones feel insecure for themselves and their families. This book may, therefore, be of help to the enlightened citizens to understand what are the controls over public finance in existence, which of them have been circumvented and how.

Index